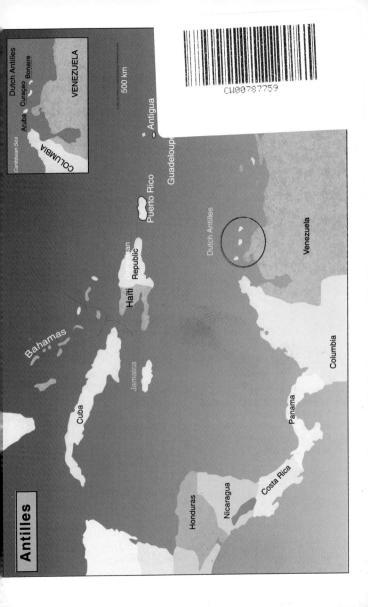

Antilles

Inset map (top):
Dutch Antilles
Aruba Curaçao Bonaire
VENEZUELA
Caribbean Sea
COLUMBIA

500 km

CW00787759

Main map labels:
Bahamas
Cuba
Jamaica
Haiti
Dominican Republic
Puerto Rico
Antigua
Guadeloupe
Dutch Antilles
Venezuela
Honduras
Nicaragua
Costa Rica
Panama
Columbia

Current practical information is essential for a quality travel guide. Although every effort was made during our research to keep this guide up-to-date, prices and other information can change rapidly — sometimes within weeks. For this reason, we would be grateful for any comments, suggestions or information you might have concerning Aruba, Bonaire and Curaçao.

Hayit Publishing
Head Office
Große Telegraphenstraße 34-36
D-50676 Cologne, Germany

1st Edition 1996
ISBN: 1-874251-42-8
© copyright 1996 Hayit Publishing GB, Ltd., London/England
© copyright 1996 original version: Hayit Verlagsgruppe, Cologne/Germany

Author: Volker Pfau
Translation, Revision, Adaptation: Scott Reznik
Typesetting: Hayit Verlagsgruppe, Cologne/Germany
Photos: Volker Pfau, Mirza Hayit (101, 121)
Print: Interprint Limited, Malta
Maps: Uwe Turek

2.5/04.6/Rs/Rs//Rs

Practical Travel

Aruba
with
Bonaire and Curaçao

Hayit Publishing

Bonbini — Welcome
to the "islands under the wind"

Aruba, like its sister islands **Bonaire** and **Curaçao**, belongs to the Dutch Antilles — the "islands under the wind". And in fact, the wind blows constantly on these islands, pleasantly refreshing. Perpetual sunshine and high temperatures make for summer throughout the year, so to speak. A fresh breeze is by all means a welcome relief.

Visitors are also welcome here on these islands with a great deal to offer. Relaxation and recreation, for example, can be found in abundance on **Aruba's** beautiful beaches but also in the elegant hotels with their superior service. And how about a visit to the casino during the evening hours? Or maybe a stroll along a secluded, moonlit beach? Fascinating excursions draw visitors to the island with natural beauty — interesting caves, bizarre rock formations and typically Caribbean landscapes — but also points of interest like the striking lighthouse and the historical fortress.

Exciting tours also entice visitors into a wetter element: By submarine, even non-divers can experience the colourful underwater world of the reefs.

And everywhere, the island's link with tradition becomes apparent: a windmill on the roadside or Dutch façades along the harbour make for Aruba's special flair.

And after having experienced Aruba, there's more worth discovering on its sister islands:

With a more peaceful ambience on **Bonaire,** visitors can delve into the wonderful diving areas, observe the flamingos and a rare species of deer in the nature reserve. Nature at its best is Bonaire's capital asset — including, of course, its beautiful beaches.

Curaçao offers more action — especially the main town of Kralendijk with its floating market and historical district, offering a lively atmosphere. A look into the manufacture of the blue Curaçao liqueur could prove interesting as well.

Highlights on the ABC Islands

The good life – on the beach under the palms
What does Caribbean bring to mind? Beautiful beaches of course; beaches bordering the emerald sea under the deep blue sky. Aruba and its sister islands have plenty of beaches which fit this image perfectly.

Recreation and action
The most beautiful diving areas on earth lie around the ABC islands: a fascinating underwater world. But other sports and recreation opportunities are available as well: surfing, sailing and much more.

History comes to life
Windmills, gabled façades, organ grinders ... sometimes, visitors could think they're in old Holland. But the defiant fort, historical districts and many more sights also bear witness to a turbulent history.

Cocktails and Carnival – Caribbean flair
A typically Caribbean atmosphere envelops visitors each and every day: a cool drink at the beach bar, barbecues under palms and spicy rhythms are not only heard during Carnival or "when the rooster is buried" on St. John's Day.

Nature and other beauties
The attraction of the ABC islands is not lush tropical vegetation. Still, nature does have something to offer: trees which grow towards the wind, bizarre rock formations, nature reserves and landscapes reminiscent of the Wild West.

Contents

Aruba

Aruba's Cities: An Overview

Bonaire

Curaçao

Using this Book

■ Books in the *Practical Travel* series offer a wealth of concrete, travel-relevant information. The most important details for your travels are clearly structured alphabetically. Cross-references ease locating the appropriate entry.

■ With travel guides in the *Practical Travel* series, information is available before the trip begins, offering details on entering the country, travel documents, the nicest beaches and accommodation options.

■ Nature lovers, sun worshippers and sports enthusiasts alike will certainly get their money's worth from the ABC islands. The coral reefs surrounding the islands are a virtual paradise for scuba diving fans. This book will accompany you to all the interesting places, offering relevant addresses to find the best and most economical options available.

■ Chapters on geography, history, culture and religion offer interesting information which will make the holiday go far beyond the superficial.

■ Practical tips will help you gain orientation fast, for everything from travel to shopping all the way to entertainment. Whether you prefer roughing it in a simple guest house or enjoy the amenities of luxury accommodation, you'll find just the right tips in *Practical Travel: Aruba*.

ARUBA

California
Lighthouse
Arashi Beach

Boca Cura

Shipwreck

Palm Beach

✝Alto-Vista-
●Chapel
Noord

Eagle Beach

✝St.-Anna Church
●

Bushiribana
Gold Smelting
Plant

Boca Andicuri

De Olde
Molen

Natural Bridge

Ayo

Druif Beach

Casibari

Arikok
National Park

Oranjestad

Santa Cruz

Boca Prins

D
e

P
a
l
m

R
e
e
f

I
s
l
a
n
d

Balashi-
Gold Smelting
Plant

Jamanota ▲

The caves

Rincon

Savaneta

Santo Largo Beach

San Nicolas

*Boca
Grande*

Seroe
Colorado

Baby Beach

Caribbean Sea

Aruba

Accommodation

There are hotels in every category on Aruba — from cheap hotels like Hotel Victoria in Oranjestad ($12/£7.20 per night) which also rents out rooms by the hour, all the way to the Hyatt Regency Hotel which, with its waterfall and wonderful gardens, is considered one of the most beautiful hotels in the world. The first hotel was built on the island in 1894; in 1993, the government registered over 500,000 tourists and in the near future, this figure will climb to 600,000. The government is now thinking differently and is attempting to hold this growth in check. It is becoming increasingly difficult to find trained personnel. The local workforce has been pretty much exhausted *(→ Economy),* and hiring workers from other islands causes problems.

Most hotels form a chain lining the beaches along the eastern coast. With its warm, blue-green water and palm trees, this coast can fulfill any tourist's classic expectation of the Caribbean.

"High Rise Hotels" and "Low Rise Hotels"

Generally speaking, the hotels are divided into two groups according to location: the row of **low rise hotels** begins right at the northern edge of Oranjestad with the *Divi Tamarijn.* After that come the *Casa del Mar,* the *Aruba Beach Club,* the *Manchebo Beach Resort,* the *Bucuti,* the *Costa Linda,* the *La Quinta complex,* the *La Cabaña,* and the row ends with the *Amsterdam Manor.* The beach in front of these hotels is called *Palm Beach (→ Beaches and Swimming).* Some of these hotels do not lie directly on the beach but are separated from the snowy white sand and turquoise water by a street.

The row of **high rise hotels** begins and ends with an eyesore: in the south is the unfinished *Ramada Renaissance Hotel.* Construction was halted when the developer went bankrupt. The government plans to use this empty building as a school to train hotel personnel. The high rise row continues with the *Aruba Royal Resort,* the *Hilton,* the *Aruba Palm Beach Hotel,* the *Golden Tulip Hotel,* the *Americana,* the *Hyatt Regency,* the *Playa Linda* and presently ends with the *Holiday Inn.* However, construction is to continue to the north. The first is the abandoned *Beta Hotels* project. It was abandoned after several millions flowed into dark channels. What is to be done with the building shell has not yet been determined. Possibly, this will also become a school for hotel staff or the building will become a supply station for the last hotel in the row, the *Marriot.* Both options are presently being discussed. The Marriot Hotel project was also endangered, but the government then took over the project. Further hotels are not to be permitted.

All hotels in both rows have high standards. Service is emphasised. This is the reason the staff is trained in specialised schools, which is not always the case in many countries. However, this is coupled with relatively high prices. Aruba is popular with American tourists for honeymoon trips. All of the hotels have special honeymoon suites.

Private Accommodation

One less expensive alternative to the hotels is private accommodation, available seemingly everywhere. Private persons, especially in Malmok, offer rooms there, some with a view of the sea. During the off-season, from April 15 to December 15, a room with a double bed can be had starting at $35 (£21) per night. A list of those offering private accommodation is available from the Aruba Tourism Authority by mail or fax.
→ *Tourism Office*

Individual Bookings

In modern times of fax communication, some might want to take the initiative in organising their own accommodation. Those who do should be aware that the official prices quoted (even after arriving on Aruba) are very high, starting at $80 (£48). Prices are generally for a double room. Prices for private accommodation are not necessarily lower than package tour options, making a package tour probably the most economical alternative.

During high season, from December 15 into April, don't count on any price reductions. Most often, hotels are completely booked — in international comparison, Aruba has high utilisation of its capacity. In cases other than this, it is good to have polished bargaining skills.

It is by all means better to book half-board. Aruba's restaurants are relatively expensive.

The Large Hotels on Aruba

Americana Aruba Beach Resort, L. G. Smith Blvd. 83, Fax: 23 191. High rise hotel, 419 rooms in two buildings, located directly on the sea, swimming pool, pool bar, three bars, three restaurants, casino, shops, tennis courts.

Amsterdam Manor Beach Resort, L.G. Smith Blvd. 252, Fax: 71 463. Low rise hotel, 47 rooms, some with kitchenette, beach across the street (not very nice; nicer beaches are five minutes' walk in either direction) swimming pool, bar, restaurant, tennis court.

Aruba Beach Club, L. G. Smith Blvd. 52, Fax: 25 557. Low rise hotel, 133 rooms, swimming pool, children's pool, pool bar, two restaurants, shops, tennis courts.

Best Western Bucuti Beach Resort, L. G. Smith Blvd. 57, Fax: 25 272. Low rise hotel, 63 rooms and suites with kitchenette, nice gardens situated on Aruba's largest and nicest section of beach.

Best Western Manchebo & Beach Resort, L. G. Smith Blvd. 55, Fax: 33 667. Low rise hotel at the southern entrance to Oranjestad, no swimming beach nearby, nice gardens, two swimming pools, three restaurants, bar.

Caribbean Palm Village Resort, Noord 43E, Fax: 62 380. Nice complex inland on Palm Beach Road where an increasing number of hotels are being built, around a ten-minute walk to the high rise hotel beach nearest to the Hyatt Regency; 170 rooms and suites, nice gardens, two swimming pools, pool bar, two restaurants, bar, tennis courts, squash courts, children's play area.

Casa Del Mar Beach Resort, J. E. Irausquin Blvd. 51, Fax: 23 000. Low rise hotel, 147 rooms and suites, all with kitchenette, swimming pool, restaurant, bar, fitness centre, laundry facilities, shops, very elegant complex.

Costa Linda Beach Resort, L. G. Smith Blvd. 59, Fax: 36 040. Low rise hotel, 155 suites with two or three bedrooms, kitchenette, swimming pool, children's pool, tennis courts, fitness centre, several restaurants, bar, night-club.

Tamarijn Aruba Beach Resort, L. G. Smith Blvd. 41, Fax: 24 150. Low rise hotel, 236 rooms, completely renovated in the spring of 1994; swimming pool, two restaurants, bars, diagonally across the street is the Alhambra Shopping Centre with shops and a supermarket.

Divi Divi Aruba Beach Resort, L. G. Smith Blvd. 47, Fax: 23 300. Low rise hotel, 203 rooms, nice gardens, two swimming pools, restaurants, bar, tennis courts, diagonally across from the Alhambra Shopping Centre.

Divi Village, L. G. Smith Blvd. 49, Fax: 35 000. Low rise hotel, 47 apartments, the beach lies across the street, swimming pool, restaurant, bar.

Dutch Village, L. G. Smith Blvd. 45, Fax: 24 150. Low rise hotel, beach across the street, 97 apartments with one or two bedrooms, swimming pool, tennis courts, restaurants, bars.

Harbourtown Beach Resort, L. G. Smith Blvd. 9, Fax: 25 317. Hotel complex directly in Oranjestad, 250 apartments, private beach; restaurants, bars and casino are only several metres away in the Harbourtown Shopping Centre.

Hilton Hotel, J. E. Irausquin Blvd. 77, Fax: 68 217. High rise hotel directly on the beach, 481 rooms and suites, 9 restaurants and bars, casino, tennis courts, shops.

Holiday Inn Aruba Beach Resort, L. G. Smith Blvd. 230, Fax: 23 600. High rise hotel directly on the beach, 600 rooms, swimming pool, conference rooms, restaurants, bars, night-club, casino, small shopping centre.

Hyatt Regency Aruba Resort & Casino, L. G. Smith Blvd. 85, Fax: 61 682. High rise hotel, 360 rooms and suites, gardens and huge swimming pool with waterfall (worth seeing), conference rooms, restaurants and cafés, bars, night-club, casino, fitness centre, tennis courts.

La Cabaña Beach Resort, L. G. Smith Blvd. 250, Fax: 75 474. Low rise hotel, 441 suites with one or two bedrooms, all with kitchenette, swimming pool, children's pool and playground, pool bar, bars, restaurants, conference rooms, night-club, fitness centre, squash courts, shops, casino (the largest in the Caribbean), entertainment; separated from the beach by the street.

Manchebo Resort has Aruba's broadest and most beautiful beach

La Quinta Beach Resort, L. G. Smith Blvd. 228, Fax: 76 263. Low rise hotel, 130 suites with one or two bedrooms, two swimming pools, restaurant, bar, night-club, tennis courts, small supermarket; the beach is across the street.

The Mill Condominium Resort, L. G. Smith Blvd., Fax: 77 271. High rise hotel, 89 apartments and suites, swimming pool, children's pool, bar, restaurant, two tennis courts, jogging trail, fitness centre, laundry facilities. The complex is situated in the second row of hotels, separated from the beach by a street and another row of hotels.

Radisson Aruba Caribbean Resort, L. G. Smith Blvd. 81, Fax: 67 316. High rise hotel, 406 rooms and suites, large garden, swimming pools, three restaurants, bars, night-club, tennis courts, shops, casino.

Sonesta Hotel, L. G. Smith Blvd. 82, Fax: 34 389. Hotel in Oranjestad, directly on the yacht harbour, 302 rooms and suites, swimming pool, private island with all facilities necessary *(→ Sights / De Palm Island)* two restaurants, three bars, night-club, conference rooms and ballrooms, fitness centre, tennis courts. The hotel is built above Oranjestad's central shopping centre with 85 shops. Guests are shuttled to De Palm Island free of charge throughout the day.

Sunset Villas, Palm Beach 33, Fax: 61 120. Apartment complex inland on Palm Beach Road which is developing into a tourist centre in Noord. Around a ten-minute walk to the beach near the Hyatt Regency Hotel. 16 rooms with kitchenette, swimming pool.

Animals and Wildlife

The first question of many visitors planning to spend their holidays on the beach is often: "Are there any sharks?" — Yes, there are, but they are on the "other side" of the island off the eastern coast. There has been no single accident involving a shark ever reported on Aruba.

Other animals on the island: in the air are a variety of colourful **birds.** Over 170 species can be found on Aruba; around 50 of these also nest on the island. The dwarf parrots are striking. The *pirkichi* in its vivid green squawks so loud that they are as difficult to overhear as they are to oversee. They enjoy staying in one spot. In contrast, a true treat to the ear is the song of the orange and yellow *trupial.* If a small bird with a yellow breast should land on your breakfast table to peck at the crumbs (and even more of a treat, the sugar), then this is a *barika.*

A beautiful sight: the brown *pelicans* sailing over the water. These are best observed at Fisherman's Hut. There, they often sit lazily for hours with the seagulls on the fishing boats. This can stink quite a bit after this ritual. It is possible to go up close to the birds (the water is very shallow there) to take a picture. From time to time, they take to flight, soaring in place because of the winds and then take a nose-dive into the sea to catch a fish. Most attempts are in vain. Only with one out of ten nose-dives does a pelican actually catch a fish. Another good place to observe birds is in the area south of the Olde Molen, the old windmill (→ *Sights*). Behind the low rise hotels (→ *Accommodation*) is a swamp area. There, cormorants and cranes can be found.

On the ground, one will notice the numerous **lizzards;** seven species can be found on Aruba. They feed on insects and plants. The largest are the *iguanas;* some of these have become quite tame, which does not always prove good for them since some people view iguanas as a culinary delicacy. One iguana with better luck is Ziggy, which lives in a palm tree near Roger's Windsurf. If he is hungry, then he stops by. His favourite foods are bananas and grapes. The name "Ziggy" was given to him because of his bizarre 'hairdo', similar to Ziggy Marley's.

There are also *scorpions* on Aruba; however, these can be seen only rarely. The normal precautions like hiking through rough terrain with good shoes and stomping to drive off these shy creatures are recommended. If having left shoes or clothing on the ground, be sure to check for unwanted guests before putting them back on. These precautions also apply to the snakes living on Aruba. One is the small and harmless *santero* snake. However, it is not a good idea to handle one of these snakes because then they do bite. Much more dangerous is the bite of the *rattlesnake,* which also lives on Aruba. It does not use its rattle as a warning, however, so it can't be heard. Rattlesnakes live exclusively in the triangle formed by San Nicolas, Fontein and Jamanota. Those who want to by all means see one can best find one south of the Jamanota mountain. If having gone a bit to close and been bitten by a rattlesnake, get to a hospital as quickly as possible to have an injection of antiserum.

Banks

On Aruba, there are numerous banks, most of which are in Oranjestad. The most easily accessible are in the shopping centre near the "Sonesta Hotel" or on the main street (Caya G. F. Croes). Banks are usually open from 8 am to noon and 1:30 to 4 pm; small variations are possible. Banks generally remain closed on Saturdays, Sundays and holidays. Exchanging currency or traveller's cheques into US dollars or florin is no problem.

Most banks, like the **Interbank** near the two supermarkets "Pueblo" and "Ling & Sons" around 150 yards into the city on the left-hand side, also exchange Eurocheques. The banks charge 2.50 florin commission per transaction regardless of the amount exchanged. For bank transactions, be sure to bring along a passport or some form of identification.

Beaches and Swimming

Sheer endless, white beaches, secluded or bustling with activity; clear, turquoise water with palms swaying in the wind — visitors will find all of this on Aruba. Aruba offers a bit of everything. Even though the palms have been planted (the dry climate allows only shrubs and cactuses to grow wild) this does not distract from their beauty.

The crystal clear water and in part dazzlingly white sand are authentically natural. The beaches' most attractive aspect: they are all accessible free of charge; none are privately owned or belong to hotels. In contrast to other Caribbean islands, the beaches are all easily accessible. And no hotel employees will say a word when non-guests go through a hotel complex to a beach and are even greeted with a friendly hello.

■ **Eagle Beach** extends in front of the low rise hotels *(→ Accommodation)*. It begins shortly after the northern entrance to Oranjestad in front of the

Ziggy, the tame iguana, gets hold of a treat

Divi-Divi Hotel complex and ends in the north near Hotel Amsterdam Manor. The area in front of the Manchebo Beach Resort is very popular. This beach extends from the hotel, from the last shady palm to the water around 80 metres (87 yards) in width. What is a magnificent sight can lose its attraction in the heat when walking barefoot on the scorching sand. Be sure to bring along sandals. All in all, Eagle Beach is rather peaceful; the huge beach offers all the beach-goers ample room. Only the jetskiiers at the northern end of Eagle Beach near the Amsterdam Manor Hotel and the Cabaña complex can be a disturbance.

■ **Palm Beach** lies in front of the high rise hotels, beginning in the south at the black block of the Ramada Renaissance Hotel complex, or rather its ruins, and ends in the north around the Holiday Inn. This portion of the beach has more action. Contributing to this is the density of the hotels with large numbers of rooms, the beach bars and the watersports facilities. The lounge chairs and beach towels are closer together in this section.

Enjoyment on the beach — almost always with a refreshing breeze

■ **Fisherman's Hut** begins north of Palm Beach. Although there are two hotels nearby (construction on the Marriot Hotel has once again commenced; the Beta Hotel project is bankrupt and there are considerations whether the building should be torn down or turned into an educational facility for hotel management), this section of beach is not suitable for swimming. It is reserved for windsurfers and fishing.

■ Two additional beaches can be found almost on Aruba's northern point towards the California Lighthouse. These are popular with local residents during the weekends; during the week, they are almost deserted. The first, **Boca Catalina,** is especially good for snorkelling *(→ Sports and Recreation),* since the small rock formations attract numerous fish. It is a popular destination for excursion boats near the *"Antilla"* shipwreck *(→ Sights).*

■ **Arashi Beach** is especially good for children. This is the last section of beach to the north, where the normal roadway ends. The beach slopes off gradually into the water: ideal for parents who don't want to worry about their children. The swimming area is also marked off by buoys.

■ Also highly appropriate for small children (as the name indicates) is **Baby Beach** on the island's southern point beyond San Nicolas and the ghost town → *Seroe Colorado.* Only during the weekends will beach-goers meet up with local residents here; otherwise, the beach is most often deserted. Travelling to Baby Beach seems like an endless journey. By car, head towards San Nicolas, then follow the signs to Seroe Colorado and turn off towards the coast to continue to Baby Beach. Along the decaying tennis courts, a small road leads to Aruba's southern tip with Baby Beach. The sand and water are clear. The refinery's rusting smokestack makes for a strange sight and may not fit the ideal image of a tropical paradise.

■ **Boca Grandi** on the opposite side of the island in the southeast is not at all suitable for children. Usually, huge waves pound the beach making for tricky and outright dangerous currents. No one cleans this beach so that there is trash lying around. Only local surfers and windsurfers can be found here occasionally, mostly during weekends.

Buses

Those who wish to explore the island of Aruba must either take an organised island tour or rent a car. Although it seems that buses are constantly underway, these are mainly on the route from Oranjestad to San Nicolas or they run along the large hotels to the end of the hotel tract at Palm Beach. Beach tourists staying in the large hotels and mainly looking for relaxation on the beach, going only occasionally into Oranjestad for shopping or a stroll will find the bus service adequate.

Bus Routes on Aruba

Each hour, three buses run from Oranjestad to the hotels and back: every hour on the hour, *Line 2 "Santa Cruz"* sets off from 6 am to 8 pm.. Later, around 9:40 and 10:40 pm, a bus leaves from the terminal in Oranjestad on Zoutman Straat right behind the Village Mall up the street to the right. All buses, even those mentioned below, reach the bus stop in front of "Wendy's" on L. G. Smith Blvd. across from the market stands around five minutes later. This is where most of the passengers board the bus. The second route between the hotels and Oranjestad is *Line 1 "Dakota"*. Every 20 minutes before the hour, the bus departs from the terminal from 5:40 am to 9:40 pm and once more at 11:40 pm. The latter bus does not operate regularly despite the schedules. But there is an occasional bus at 10:40 pm which does not appear on the official schedules at all.

An additional route, the *"Palm Beach"* line, mainly serves the "low and high rise hotels" along the beach. The bus departs every half hour from Oranjestad. Taking the bus in Aruba is still an adventure despite these three bus routes.

Bus connections are particularly bad for those tourists staying in the guest houses in Malmok in the island's north. Only one bus line, the *"Basiruti"* or *"Malmok"*, provides service to the hotels, running once an hour between Oranjestad and Malmok. The bus departs for the main terminal 20 minutes past the hour and arrives at the island's northern point in Basiruti on the hour. The last bus to Malmok departs definitively at 10:20 pm. Most often, these buses are only identified by a small sign above the dashboard.

No matter which destination, it is always best to ask for assistance. The local residents are generally glad to help and the bus drivers are also willing to provide assistance. They speak English.

Passengers board the bus at the front and pay the driver. A single trip costs $1 (60p) or 1.75 florin. Round trip costs $1.75 (£1.05) or 3 florin. Often, the front and rear doors remain open during the trip as do all the windows, the wind whipping through the bus. The bus stops are officially marked and in the city centre and in front of the large hotels, there are bus stop shelters. Outside the cities in rural areas, there is an occasional, unobtrusive yellow sign reading "bus stop 12m". Would-be passengers can stop a bus by waving. The 'friedly wave technique' works everywhere except in the cities, even where there are no bus stop signs. In the older bus models, there is a black button between the windows every second row of seats. Passengers wanting the bus driver to stop at the next bus stop must press these. In newer buses, a rubber strip running above the windows replaces the buttons.One word of caution: the bus drivers often brake abruptly.

Camping

Camping is more or less unheard-of on Aruba. The least expensive accommodation option is provided by guest houses (→ *Accommodation*). It is by no means a good idea to set up camp just anywhere in the wilderness because the police will not take long to find a pitched tent.

Upon entering Aruba, campers run the risk of being denied entry and at the very least, they will have significant difficulties with the officials. Visitors with a backpack are asked especially pointedly which hotel they have booked.

Car Rental

There is meanwhile an incredible number of car rental agencies on Aruba. At the airport alone are nineteen rental agencies, all of them competing with 'unbelievable offers'.

In reality, all are offering pretty much the same: cars, compact cars. mid-sized cars, jeeps and convertibles.

The minimum rental period is four hours. The lowest price for a compact car is around $30 (£18) per day and $180 (£108) per week (making for one day of 'free' driving for the price of six (Happy Island Rent-a-Car). It is worthwhile bargaining with the prices for those renting in excess of two weeks. The individual agencies can be found in the airport building; among these are Hertz and AVIS where it is possible to reserve a car from home. The cars are in good condition.

Telephone Numbers of Car Rental Agencies

ACE, Tel: 76 373 or 30 840
Airways, Tel: 21 845
Aruba Rent a Car, Tel: 31 020
Budget, Tel: 28 600 or 23 230
Caribbean Car Rental, Tel: 29 118
Courtesy Car Rental, Tel: 26 757
Deals on Wheels, Tel: 34 042
Econo, Tel: 35 010
Five Star, Tel: 27 600
Happy Island, Tel: 35 236
Hedwina Car Rental, Tel: 26 442
Hertz/De Palm Tours, Tel: 24 400
Marco's Car Rental, Tel: 25 295
Optima Rent a Car, Tel: 35 622
Thrifty Car Rental, Tel: 35 335
Toyota Rent a Car, Tel: 34 832

Renting a Car — What to Note

The procedure of renting a car is simple with a credit card: pick up the phone, ask what's offered, order a car. The rental company will deliver the car to the hotel. The renter is given the keys upon presenting proof that he or she is at least 21 years of age and holds a valid driving licence. Be sure to make a note in the contract of any damage already present (include a sketch of the vehicle). Inspect the car before signing the contract and set an exact date and time when the car is to be returned. When paying by credit card, the signed receipt is the deposit in case something does happen to the vehicle. If all goes well and the car is returned undamaged, the final amount is entered in the contract and everything is taken care of.

Casinos

It is the simplest thing in the world to get rid of money on Aruba. This is not only a reflection of Caribbean prices, but also results from the casinos. Meanwhile, there are no less than twelve casinos on the island. If it was gold earlier and later oil which attracted those in search of a quick fortune, now it is the casinos. Those who come across tourists carrying paper cups filled with coins in Oranjestad can be certain these are tourists headed for or coming from a casino.

Most of the large hotels have their own casinos and most open in the morning for the early gamblers. The slot machines spin into action as early as 11 am; tables open around 1 pm. The casinos first close when the last gambler loses interest. The gamblers at the 'hot tables' challenge lady luck until late at night or even into the early morning. Visitors to casinos must be at least 18 years of age.

The one-armed bandits await their chance to swallow coins — nickels, quarters, half-dollars and dollars. For other games, the minimum bet is usually a dollar. A bulletin board usually displays a 'board of fame' with pictures of lucky visitors with the money and cars they took home with them tax-free.

Whether the visitor is interested in roulette, blackjack, craps, baccarat, slot machines or simply in observing the goings-on, attire seems irrelevant. At least, visitors are not asked to leave if they are casually dressed. Some visitors spend hour after hour in front of the slots dressed in beach attire. No one complains officially about this. However, in the informational tourist advertising brochures, it is noted that dressing up in the evening is a sign of respect. By the way: Arubans are only allowed into a casino four times each year.

Limited Luck at the Slots

Armed with masses of coins, visitors plop themselves in front of the one-armed bandits. What the goal of the game is, is displayed on the machine. This is usually getting three identical symbols. Winnings vary depending on the symbols and the jackpot. And sometimes, lady luck does smile: those who hit the jackpots should have a bucket ready for all the coins.

■ Roulette

The chances of winning in roulette are better than in the lottery, so I've heard. A large sum of money can be won in a single game. The highest winnings, and with this the highest risk, is placing a bet on one number. Bets may be placed only when the croupier says so and only up to the point he declares "Rien ne va plus" (no more bets), as the marble moves towards the numbers. If the ball indeed lands on the 'lucky number' then this pays 35 to 1. Those who bet on two numbers (by simply placing the chip or chips on the line between two numbers) win 17 times what they bet. Bets on three numbers pay 11 to 1 and bets on four numbers, 8 to 1. And it doesn't stop there: on the spots along the columns, players can bet on six, twelve or 24 numbers simultaneously. The payoff sinks as the numbers bet on increase, from 5 to 1 to $1\frac{1}{2}$ to 1. In addition, players can bet on red (rouge) or black (noir); on even (pair) or odd (impair) numbers.

■ Blackjack

Players place their bets and are dealt two cards. All players play against the dealer or croupier. The object is to get as close to 21 as possible, the best hand being exactly 21. Those who go over, lose. Face cards count as ten while number cards count their value. An ace can be either 1 or 11. The croupier, or dealer, begins the game by dealing two cards. Players can then be dealt more cards to reach 21. The dealer must take a card if he is below 17.

■ Craps

For the novice gambler, craps appears rather complicated; beginners will probably have to chalk up a number of lost bets to experience. However, craps is one of the most exciting casino games, and watching it being played is interesting. One player against everyone else is often the motto. The following is a brief summary of the most important rules of craps: the table has a high edge and one player rolls two dice; the other players bet either for or against him. If the player rolling the dice gets a 7 or 11, he wins — and all the players who bet for him or her (the *pass line* on the edge of the playing field). If the player rolls a two, a three or a twelve, then he or she loses; and those who placed their bets on the *don't pass line* win. If the player rolls any other number, then he or she must roll this number again before rolling a seven. Otherwise, he or she loses. *Come* is the term for those who believe the player will accomplish this; *don't come* for those who think the player will roll a 7 first.

■ Baccarat

Baccarat is a variation on blackjack; the object of the game is to reach nine points. The dealer deals two cars for the players and the bank. Then, the dealer deals more cards if desired. Tens and face cards count as zero; an ace, as one point. The other cards count as their face value. Others can bet on the player, the bank or undecided. Six players can play at once.

Cinema

Aruba hardly has any drive-in theatres. One drive-in has been in operation on Aruba for 25 years and is very popular. Every evening, current US feature films are presented on the huge screen in the original language. Some have Spanish subtitles. For those who would enjoy an evening at the drive-in, admission is $3 (£1.80) or 5 florin for adults and $2 (£1.20) or 3 florin for children. The drive-in has 350 parking spaces and the aroma of popcorn from

the snack bar fills the air. The film changes every week on Friday. Announcements can be found in the newspapers "Bon Dia Aruba" and "Diario".
The sound transmission is interesting: it functions using the car radio because the drive-in has two radio stations of its own which can be received on 95.7 FM or 1540 AM. If the radio doesn't work, drive-in visitors can hang two speakers on the side windows. If this is necessary, be sure to arrive early since not all of the speakers work and there aren't any at all at some places. The show begins daily at 8:30 pm except on Fridays and Saturdays which have two showings at 8 and 10:30 pm.
The drive-in is located south of Oranjestad next to the 1B road towards San Nicolas and there are as good as no signs for it.

> *Directions from the hotels:* First, drive towards the airport, continuing towards San Nicolas. Past the road which crosses a bridge, continue to the first traffic light after the airport. There, turn left towards 4B Paradera / St. Cruz. After around 250 metres (275 yards), turn right and drive along a green fence to the driveway leading to the drive-in.

Climate

In the local language, *Papiamento (→ Language)*, there actually couldn't be a term for bad weather. The weather is simply too beautiful throughout the year to warrant a word to the contrary. The sun shines from 7 to 9 hours a day. Due to the proximity of the equator, the sun rises at almost the same time at 6:30 am and sets spectacularly over the sea around 6:10 pm. Half an hour after sunset, the sky turns a Caribbean pink.
The average temperature on Aruba (measured both day and night) is 27.8°C (82°F). The daily high varies throughout the year from 30°C (86°F) to 33°C (91°F) and from 24°C (75°F) to 26°C (79°F) is the nightly 'low'. Without the constant northeasterly trade winds, which serve as a type of natural air conditioning, the heat on the island would be unbearable. Aruba lies outside the hurricane zone; tropical storms have never reached Aruba's shores. The turquoise sea is as warm as a bathtub all year long; the low water temperatures 'drop' to 25°C (77°F) while the high is around 28°C (82°F).
The average annual precipitation on Aruba is around 450 millimetres (17$\frac{1}{2}$ inches). The rains fall, if at all, only briefly but heavily during the months of October (65mm/2$\frac{1}{2}$ inches), November (94mm/3$\frac{3}{4}$ inches) and December (79mm/3 inches). After five to ten minutes, the rain shower is usually over. The hottest months are August, September and October. → *Clothing*

Clothing

For Aruba, the 'light sweater for cool evenings' can be left at home. T-shirts, short sleeved shirts, light blouses, Bermuda shorts and short skirts are completely sufficient. Those who enjoy dressing up in a suit or evening dress can do this but it is not a must. Some tourists even visit the casinos and restaurants in beach attire and tennis shoes. The local residents refer to this attire as *'barefoot elegance'.* However, proper attire for the evening is appreciated. During the rainy season from November to January, a light rain jacket for the brief showers lasting 10 to 15 minutes can prove useful.

Cuisine, Food and Drink

Self-Catering

Every day, small ships packed with meat, fruit and vegetables from Venezuela and Columbia land at Oranjestad's harbour. These items are then sold by the fishermen and merchants at the *Schooner Market* right next door. A butcher

Tropical fruits in abundance — and fresh every day!

can also be found in the middle of the row of market stands. At the market, a bit of bargaining with the prices can ensure the shopper the best prices for fruits and vegetables. In addition, the supermarkets offer a wide selection of groceries, often imported from the US.

Eating Habits

There is no special "breakfast culture" on Aruba: tea, water, sometimes coffee and a sandwich — this is how most locals begin their day. The main meal of the day is lunch. A *soppi di banana* (banana soup), a *soppi die cabritu* (mutton soup), a *soppi die Galinja* (chicken soup) or a *soppi die* pisca (fish soup) begins the meal. The soups are more like stews than broth. As the second course, a fish or meat dish follows. Local residents mostly eat chicken or mutton. Cattle and goats first came to Aruba with oil refinery workers recruited from numerous nations. Pot roast, called stobá is popular on Aruba. This is prepared in many variations, usually with mutton or lamb and vegetables, herbs and spices. However, chicken or pork is also prepared in this way.

For supper, a small warm meal is usually served, often made up of leftovers from the midday meal. Another option is to eat a sandwich again or a *pastchi,* a pastry filled with meat or fish.

Pan bati a type of flatbread made from flour, maize (corn), milk and salt plays an important role in Aruban cuisine. It is often served along with the meal in good restaurants.

Funchi is porridge made from cornmeal, salt and butter cooked in boiling water. Funchi is served with butter as a side dish along with the main course. In the late evening, local residents enjoy visiting one of the many snack bars if they feel somewhat hungry. The "white trucks", literally trucks painted white, serving local specialities are also very popular.

Hotel Cuisine

For breakfast, the larger hotels mostly have buffets. Eggs prepared in every way, ham, cheese, sausages, bacon, fried potatoes, pancakes, syrup, various types of bread, jam, fruit and fruit salads... Served with the buffet are fruit juices, coffee and tea. Visitors will notice that breakfast buffets are tailored to the tastes of North American tourists. In smaller hotels, the selection is usually more limited but almost always, there is a buffet.

For lunch and dinner, those staying in larger hotels will often have a choice between two or even three restaurants with various specialities.

A more economical option is booking half or full board. Eating in restaurants, whether in hotels or elsewhere, is expensive.

Aruban Cuisine

Visitors should not expect a special and typically Aruban cuisine. Although restaurants repeatedly advertise "original Papiamento cuisine", it remains unclear what original Papiamento cuisine actually is. At the most, some dishes may be considered "typically Aruban" meaning they have been influenced by Creole cuisine. Generally speaking, the Arubans seem to have collected the most delicious foods from the world in the composition of their island's cuisine. And this is understandable considering the numerous immigrants from just as numerous nations.

Those who do not enjoy cooking themselves will certainly not starve: there is one restaurant after the next on Aruba. Most serve steaks and fish dishes. Salads are less common.

Some Delicious Caribbean Recipes

Chicken Stew with Bananas

Ingredients: One chicken (giblets removed), one leek stalk, one cooking banana, two carrots, one bunch of mixed herbs, one onion, two celery stalks, two bay leaves, two cloves, salt, peppercorns, sherry.

Preparation: Place the chicken in saltwater and bring to a boil. The chicken should be just covered by the water. Cook the chicken for around 30 minutes. Add the washed and diced vegetables along with the herbs. After another hour, the meat should fall from the bones. Remove the chicken from the broth and strain the broth. Return to a boil. Peel the banana by cutting off both ends and slice lengthwise; remove the peel. Slice the banana and add to the broth. Bone the chicken and dice the meat. Slice the leek and add it to the stew along with the meat. Season with spices and add sherry to taste.

Preparation time including cooking time: around two hours.

Shrimps Flambé

Ingredients: 1 lb. shrimps, 4 tablespoons butter, fresh sliced mushrooms, 1 small diced onion, three garlic cloves, minced parsley, 1 teaspoon cognac, 1/2 cup heavy cream, one tablespoon roasted almond slices, salt and pepper.

Preparation: brown diced onion and add tomatoes and mushrooms; simmer briefly. Add cream and parsley. Season shrimps, sauté in butter and garlic briefly until golden brown; flambé with cognac. Add to cream mixture, bring to a boil, sprinkle with almonds. Serve hot.

Marinated Lemon Fish

Ingredients: 1 lb. filet of redfish or mackerel (fresh, not frozen), six untreated lemons, two tomatoes, one tablespoon each of minced parsley, chives and dill, two onions, two tablespoons vegetable oil, ½ teaspoon sugar, a pinch of cayenne pepper, salt.
Preparation: Wash fish, remove head and bones. Cut fish into bite-sized pieces. Cut off piece of lemon peel and slice into fine strips; mix with fish. Pour 2/3 of the lemon juice over the fish. Cover dish and marinate refrigerated overnight. The next morning, stir once more. Scald the tomatoes, peel and dice. Place in another bowl, add fish and sprinkle herbs over the mixture. Peel onions and cut into fine slices. Combine remaining lemon juice with oil, sugar, cayenne pepper and salt; mix well. Cover bowl and marinate for half a day. The marinated fish should be served chilled. The chilled fish can also be served with boiled potatoes and salad.

Creole Pork

Ingredients: 1¼ lb. pork scallops or chops (bones removed), two garlic cloves, a dash of caraway, salt, pepper, 2 tablespoons vinegar, 4 tablespoons vegetable oil, two large onions, one red bell pepper, paprika.
Preparation: Cut meat into thin strips, mince garlic and mix with caraway, salt, pepper, paprika, vinegar and oil. Marinate covered in the refrigerator one to two days, stirring once. Peel and dice the onion. Wash the bell pepper and cut into thin strips. Season both with salt and pepper and sauté in oil over medium heat until tender. Remove vegetables from pan. Place the meat in the pan with the marinade and brown on both sides over high heat. Add vegetables and serve with rice. The meat may not stand long after cooking, otherwise it can get tough.

Many Arubans, but predominantly North American tourists, enjoy eating at the fast food chains: Wendy's, McDonald's, Pizza Hut, Kentucky Fried Chicken, Taco Bell... Domino's Pizza even delivers to the hotel room.

Beverages
Drinking enough liquids (non-alcoholic) is important in the Caribbean. The body loses a lot of fluids and minerals in the heat, even though this is not always noticeable because of the constant breeze. Fruit juices and water are

the best thirst quenchers. Of course, there is also a wide selection of cocktails on Aruba in every bar. Most cocktails are based on rum or Curaçao liqueur. During the day, a *Sorsaka* — a non-alcoholic cocktail made with sour fruit juice mixed with sugar, milk, cinnamon, vanilla and ice cubes — is quite refreshing. Those who enjoy beer need not forgo this refreshment. The Dutch Heineken Brewery also brews their beer on Curaçao; hops and malt are imported from Europe especially for this.

Caribbean Cocktails and Drinks

Daiquiri
1 part lime juice, 5 parts rum, 1 teaspoon sugar syrup. Shake or blend with three ice cubes. Serve with one tablespoon orange juice or Curaçao orange or grapefruit juice and maraschino.

Mai Tai
Original Trader Vic version from 1944; juice from one lime, 1 teaspoon sugar syrup, one teaspoon orange syrup, one shot Curaçao orange, 2 shots dark Jamaican rum, 2 shots Martinique rum, fresh mint sprig to garnish, serve over ice.

Piña Colada
2 shots of cream, $3\frac{1}{2}$ shots of light rum, 4 shots of coconut milk, 6 tablespoons crushed pineapple, serve over crushed ice.

Tequilla Sunrise
1 tablespoon crème de cassis, $\frac{1}{4}$ glass Curaçao orange, $\frac{1}{4}$ glass lime juice, $\frac{1}{2}$ glass tequila, ice cubes, a splash of soda water.

Captain's Morn (non-alcoholic)
1 egg yolk, 1 tablespoon sugar syrup, $\frac{1}{4}$ glass cream of coconut, $\frac{1}{4}$ glass cream, $\frac{1}{2}$ glass grape juice, shake and serve over ice cubes.

Customs Regulations

Although Aruba, Bonaire and Curaçao belong to the Kingdom of the Netherlands, custom matters are not treated as if the islands were in the EU. Those returning to Great Britain must take this into consideration. Information on customs allowances is available from your local customs authority and is usually listed in in-flight magazines aboard flights to and from Aruba.

Drinking Water

Water from the faucet on Aruba comes from the second largest salt extraction plant in the world. The water is absolutely pure and can be drunk without reservation. In some places, the water pipes are above ground or only slightly below so that the water comes out of the faucet lukewarm to warm.

The water need not be boiled and even those with sensitive stomachs need not be afraid of ice cubes in their cocktails.

In the period from 1983 to 1984 and in 1990, a total of five salt extraction plants were set up to distil sea-water into drinking water. Their capacity is sufficient to produce 34,000 cubic metres (around 1.4 million gallons) of drinking water per day.

In 1992, the daily drinking water consumption was 26,550 cubic metres (around 1.12 million gallons). Thus, an expansion of capacity will prove necessary in the near future due to the growing number of hotels, tourists and the new golf course on the island's northern point. The drinking water supply stored in huge tanks on various hills on the island is sufficient for seven to eight days.

Driving and Traffic Regulations

Solid lines obviously don't mean much for everyday traffic on Aruba; nor do speed limits. Many cars leave a very dented impression. And still: the number of traffic deaths has dropped considerably despite the drastic increase in the number of cars on the roads as is evidenced by the daily traffic jams in Oranjestad. No one has counted the individual vehicles per sé, but there will probably be as many cars on Aruba as residents very soon.

In 1993, police statistics registered eight traffic deaths. The police hypothesise that the increased traffic in recent years makes aggressive driving more difficult.

On Aruba, Traffic is on the right-hand side of the road. **Traffic signs** are standard European.

One difference can be seen in the traffic lights which switch directly from red to green with no yellow phase — like in North America. At most crossings, there are sensors, meaning that a light which just turned red can switch back to green only seconds after a car reaches the traffic light.

(→ *Fuel*)

The Drunk Driving Test — "Please touch your nose"

There is no **blood alcohol limit** on Aruba. The police intervene when a driver is obviously drunk. The driver must then complete two tests: if the police stops a driver they think has had too much to drink, the driver must stand on one foot and touch the tip of his nose with both index fingers, eyes closed. If the driver cannot do this, the second test is performed. A 'test car' is set up at the police station: a chair, a steering wheel, three pedals (the accelerator, the clutch and the brakes). The alleged drunk driver must then act as if he or she is driving. A green light begins the test. At one point, a police officer switches the green light to red — the driver hits the brakes. If the driver's reaction time is impaired, the driving licence is confiscated and a fine must be paid. One police officer put it this way: "We have 'regulars' here, who have had to take the test two or three times. Some can hardly stand but they are so experienced in taking the test that they always pass with flying colours. We have to let them go." This probably won't change in the near future according to the police officer. The police repeatedly push for a blood alcohol limit, but the

Economy

Aruba is an affluent country. Despite some difficulties, it has been possible to secure a positive economic development for the island.

One indication for Aruba's good economic standing is, for example, the rate of unemployment. In December of 1992, it was a phenomenal 0.6%. The situation on the labour market has become so drastic that trained personnel has had to be 'imported' from other Caribbean Islands. At present, the economy is predominantly dependent on tourism, a development which was intentional.

The year 1824 marked the first time Aruba was noticed in an economic sense: gold was discovered. But only 100 years later, the fever was over and gold mining was halted because the extraction was no longer economically feasible. Up to then, around 1,300 grams of fold had been discovered and extracted.

The gold fever had hardly subsided when the 'black gold fever' ran rampant: oil was discovered in Venezuela and Aruba's location and political stability were decisive factors for the Lago Oil and Transport Company to build an oil refinery on Aruba's. Eight years later, the company became a subsidiary of Esso, a brand owned by the Exxon company.

The refinery brought Aruba's population affluence for the first time. The management was first from the US and Europe but workers were recruited from the local population. Many came from other Caribbean islands to find work on Aruba at this time as well. In March 1985, one third of tax income to the island and over half of the income in foreign currencies came from Exxon. This exacerbated the shock when Exxon decided to close down the refinery on Aruba due to the drastic drop in the demand for oil. Simultaneously, the tourism industry, the island's second economic base, decayed. With the plummeting Bolivar, hardly any Venezuelan visitors came to the island. Unemployment skyrocketed to around 20%.

In this alarming situation, the mother country and the International Monetary Fund intervened: a specific economic programme was developed to spur tourism. The government secured loans for the large hotel projects, a free trade zone was established and the financial system, restructured. Within only a few years, one hotel was built after another and the Arubans found work once more. Today, there is no unemployment worth mentioning on Aruba. However, the other side of the coin is that Aruba is almost completely dependent on tourism. Presently, tourism managers are increasingly looking to Europe for new opportunities to attract visitors.

Electricity

On Aruba, the electrical supply is 110 volts alternating current at 60 Hz. The sockets are US standard. For those arriving from other regions of the world, it is a good idea to bring along adapters, especially since these are not readily available on Aruba.

Only extremely rarely is there a power failure on Aruba. Recently, the Aruban government imported a huge emergency generator.

Emergencies

Every hotel has a doctor on call for guests 24 hours a day. In emergencies, contact the reception (→ *Medical Care, Police*). Emergency phone numbers: **Ambulance/ Fire:** 115; **Police:** 111 00 or 245 55; **Hospital:** 243 00

Entering Aruba

If a larger aeroplane lands at the *Reina Beatrix Airport* on Aruba, then long lines form in front of the Immigration counters. The lines are, however, processed quickly since the procedure is short and the visitors, prepared.

During the flight, visitors are given and entry/exit card which must be filled out with name, date and place of birth, address, profession, marital status, departure airport, flight number, planned duration of stay, purpose of visit, address on the island, nationality and date of issue for the passport. Thus, the passport is needed during the flight.

For US and Canadian citizens, proof of identification in lieu of a passport will suffice (birth certificate, naturalisation papers, voter registration card, etc.) For those who do not know their address on the island since they plan on looking for something after arriving, it is sufficient to enter a well-known hotel. The entry form is then presented to the *immigration officer* along with the passport. The officer adds this to his or her files and places a copy of the card in the passport. The copy must be presented upon departure; otherwise, there could be problems.

Those planning on staying longer than the usual two or three weeks should be ready to show the return ticket since proof of return is a condition for entry. Generally, a stay lasting up to three months is possible without a residency permit. New arrivals who state "business" as their travel purpose are questioned more intensively by the immigration officers.

Excursions

Anyone on Aruba with a car either opens a rental agency or offers tours. Those with a boat use it to offer excursions — from fishing tours to moonlight cruises. In short, tourists are catered to.

The selection of excursions above and below the ground, to the water and under the sea or even in the air is huge. Tourists are virtually inundated with the continually changing selection. Those offering excursions print up flyers praising their tours. Two large companies have been able to take on market leadership thanks to their financial strength. These two companies are represented in almost every larger hotel: *De Palm Tours* (Tel: 24 400) and *Pelican Watersports* (Tel: 31 228). In part, they represent the smaller entrepreneurs described above, who predominantly organise excursions in small buses, jeeps or by mountain bike, filling those market niches left by the large companies.

A Selection of Excursions

Jeep Tour around the island: full day, around $50 (£30)

Horseback Riding: one to 2½ hours, $15 to $45 (£9 to £27)

Helicopter Tour: twenty minutes for $45 (£27), Tel: 37 667; the helicopter pad is located near the "Cabana Resort" on the 1A Street across from "Adventure Golf".

Sailing and Snorkelling: three hours for $25 (£15)
Catamaraning: two to six hours from $25 to $38 (£15 to £23)
Submarine Tour: two hours, $59 (£35); $29 (£17) for children from 4 to 12 years of age

An Underwater Adventure — A Submarine Tour

A ship brings the submarine passengers from the harbour (docked across from the "Sonesta Hotel") in Oranjestad to the "Atlantis" submarine (a small hut along the harbour which can't be missed). On the trip to the "Atlantis", passengers can take in the view of the airport and the island's dump. The "Atlantis" glides about an hour through depths around 50 metres (165 feet) along the Barcadera Reef. Forty-six passengers are seated in two rows. A porthole next to each seat offers an unobstructed view. The trip is structured so that all passengers, both on the port and starboard sides will have all seen the same things upon returning.

For underwater photography, a film speed of 400 ASA or higher is recommended. Such a trip is ideal for everyone, who wants to take in the underwater world without having to snorkel or scuba dive. *Tip:* The underwater visibility is best after a few calm days. A day with high winds and rough seas makes fur murky water. This tour can by no means be recommended for those with claustrophobia. The submarine is usually filled to capacity, especially on days when cruise ships dock in the harbour. For this reason, it is advisable to book the tour in advance. This is possible at almost every hotel reception, at the above mentioned organisers or directly by contacting Tel: 37 007 or 36 090.

Seaworld Explorer: A cross between a boat and a submarine with an arched glass bottom. $1\frac{1}{2}$ hours for $29 (£17)
Glass Bottom Boat: $1\frac{1}{2}$ hours for $15 (£9)
Simple Boat Tour: one hour for $15 (£9)
Day Trip to Caracas, Venezuela: $240 (£145)
Day Trip to Curaçao: $200 (£120)

With the two last tours mentioned, it is worthwhile to plan the trip independently or through one of the local travel agencies since this can save significantly in cost. There are also daily flights to Bonaire.

Here, a list of **local travel agents:**

Aruba Bank Travel, L. G. Smith Blvd. 105, Oranjestad, Tel: 21 553
Bon Voyage Travel, Havenstraat 5, Tel: 30 706
Discovery Travel, Harbourtown 425, Tel: 30 658

The selection of island tours can be confusing and it is constantly changing. It is best to compare the current selection using the omnipresent flyers and at the hotel reception.

Fuel

The traffic density on Aruba is reflected in the density of the service station network. For tourists, the nearest service stations are the two Esso stations at the harbour and near the high rise hotels. The service station near the entrance to Oranjestad is open around the clock. Aruba's service stations also have shops offering a number of items.

Prices: Unleaded 1.089 florin per litre (around 3.79 florin, $2.14 or £1.28 per gallon) for self-service; 1.099 florin per litre (4.15 florin, $2.35 or £1.41 per gallon) for full service.

Fuelling up on Aruba

On Aruba both full service and self-service are offered.

Be sure to note that the prices displayed on the pumps are in florin. If you pay the station attendant $20, for example, be sure that the pump stops at 35 florin (20 x 1.75 = 35 florin) and not at 20.

Some service station attendants seem to make some extra money on the side by cashing in dollars and stopping the pump at the dollar instead of florin amount.

Self-service is a little bit less expensive and fuel must be prepaid. The amount is entered into a computer and the pump runs up to the exact amount paid.

Geography

Aruba is the westernmost island in the Lesser Antilles, the "islands under the wind". Geographically, Aruba lies at 12 degrees 30 minutes north latitude and 70 degrees west longitude. With this, it lies near the equator at the same latitude as the Dominican Republic or the Cape Verde Islands off the west African coast. A strait around 30 kilometres (19 miles) wide separates the island from the Venezuelan peninsula of Paraguanà. Aruba, like its neighbours Bonaire and Curaçao belongs to the kingdom of the Netherlands (→ *History*). The island has a length of 31 kilometres (19½ miles) and is around 8 kilometres (5 miles) wide at its centre. With a total area of 193 square kilometres (75 square miles), Aruba is slightly larger than the District of Columbia or the Channel Islands of Jersey and Guernsey combined. The highest points on the islands are the 'mountains' *Jamanota* at 189 metres (618 feet) and *Arikok* at 188 metres (615 feet). Aruba's capital city is Oranjestad. Sinking air streams in the trade winds zone make for a very arid climate with average annual precipitation lying at 438 mm (slightly over 17 inches). The trade winds are the result of air pressure differences in the subtropical climatic zone towards the equator. On the northern hemisphere, the trade winds blow constantly from the northeast due to the earth's rotation. Only near the equator at around 5 degrees north latitude do they lose their strength. Aruba lies within the trade wind belt and has constant winds for this reason. The sinking warm air prevents the relatively moist air over the island from rising. At a height of around 1,000 to 1,500 metres (3,270 to 4,900 feet) the air is 'trapped', preventing rain clouds from forming. The arid → *climate* does not allow for a blanket of vegetation to cover the island. Sand and stone plateaus, large rocks, cactuses, low shrubs and bushes with hearty leaves *(→ Vegetation)* are characteristic of the island for this reason. Between Aruba, Bonaire and Curaçao, the seas' water are driven through the straits separating the islands by the easterly winds and the northern and southern equatorial currents, resulting from the earth's rotation. The currents flow along the islands and then move off north along the Central American coast where a portion veers off into the Gulf of Mexico. The larger part, however, flows along the eastern coast of the US from Florida at relatively high speeds. The Gulf Stream then veers off to the east around New York. Branches of the Gulf Stream reach Ireland, making for a relatively warm climate there.

Geographically, the Caribbean coastal zone verging on Venezuela is a young region. Over 100 million years ago, the islands' base formed through volcanic eruptions on the ocean floor and oceanic deposits. This built up the shallow, hilly landscape of the island's inland regions on which sediments and lime formations developed. During the early Tertiary period which began around 65 million years ago, coral lime was deposited around the island core and in part, on top of the developing island a 'short' time later. Around 40 million years thereafter, this base rose out of the sea. The coral banks surrounding the island continued to grow. During the Quaternary Period which began around 1.8 million years ago, the island lay significantly lower than today. The impressive coral reefs of today formed on the old rock core. Later, the island was transformed significantly by varying temperatures and sea levels. Simultaneously, Aruba was thrust upwards and tilted. The coral reefs at the islands core died off. Resulting from this lengthy process was a geomorphologic trisection of the island; the hilly core of the island is predominantly composed of basalt, the northeastern regions, of heavily weathered quartz diorite and the island's southeast, of broken limestone plateaux. Aruba has no flowing body of water on its surface. On Aruba's **western side** lie the wonderful beaches named Eagle Beach, Palm Beach and Basiruti lined with the hotels

(→ *Accommodation*).This side of the island has a flat coastline with coral banks off the coast. The **inland region** is characterised by a hilly landscape scattered with large rocks. Steps have been carved into the largest of these rocks so that they are easier to climb. The mystery of their origin or formation has yet to be solved. However, scientists postulate that they are of volcanic origin. Aruba's **eastern coast** is fringed in coastal cliffs, alternating with coral limestone and rock formations.

Large waves pound the coastline and wash out the cliffs in many places. This process led to the bizarre rock formations like the → *Natural Bridge* and *Boca Grandi*.

History

For centuries, Aruba was populated by the Arawak Indians. This was supported by archaeological finds. A few hundred of these peaceful people lived in clay huts on the barren island and eked out a paltry existence around the level of humans during the Stone Age. In 1499, the Spanish seafarer *Alonso de*

Another side of Aruba: landscapes right out of a wild west film

Ojeda, who had sailed with Christopher Columbus, discovered the islands of Curaçao and Aruba. Historians presume that Ojeda never set foot on Aruba. After the 'discovery', the Indians on Aruba were left in peace for a while. The Spaniards simply had no use for the 'Islas inútiles', the 'useless islands'. However, since workers were desperately needed on Santo Domingo in the copper mines a few years later, the Arawaks were shipped there as slaves in 1513. Fourteen years later, some of the deported Arawaks found their way back to the island where another group of Indians from Venezuela had meanwhile settled.

In addition to the Indians, the Spaniards also brought horses, donkeys, cattle, pigs, sheep, goats and chickens to Aruba. The animals were set free to roam the island in search of their own food. Several Spanish missionaries also came to the island to convert the Indians to Catholicism (→ *Religion*).

In 1633, the Spanish conquered Sint Maarten, a Dutch possession up to then, and the eight-year war between the Spanish and the Dutch reached its climax. The Dutch West India Company countered by deciding to take Curaçao from Spain. From August 21, 1634 onwards, Curaçao was under Dutch rule. Aruba and Bonaire were occupied at the same time.

Peter Struyvesant became the island's first governor; later, he would become governor of New Amsterdam, which is now New York. He developed Curaçao into the Netherlands' most important trade hub in the Caribbean.

Aruba was used by the Dutch West India Company as a 'huge pasture' so to speak, especially for horse breeding. Goats also flourished on the island (and are still there). For the most part, the Indians were left in peace. In increasing numbers, they came from the mainland since there was plenty of work on Aruba.

In 1754, the Division allowed white settlers to come to the island. From 1770 onwards, residents of Curaçao and Bonaire were also allowed to move to Aruba. The intensive breeding of horses, goats and sheep continued. Then, in 1799, the first English war ship appeared on the horizon. The Dutch answered with cannonfire and the English disappeared as suddenly as the came. In 1805, however, the English had more luck. They occupied Aruba, Bonaire and Curaçao. The Dutch did attempt to reconquer the islands, but the English knew how to use the cannons at Fort Zoutman as well.

In 1986, the oil refinery ceased processing; the governments in the Netherlands and on Curaçao desperately sought an alternative source of income, ultimately opting to promote tourism — with the best of results. In the past five years, this economic sector virtually exploded and today, tourism is the main source of income for all three islands.

The oil refinery provided work for Arubans over decades. Their living standards became higher than any other Caribbean Island. With the rising wealth, the self-esteem of the Arubans grew and, along with it, the desire for independence. Since 1948, the Arubans attempted to achieve special status in regard to their ties to the Netherlands. However, this would first come true on January 1, 1986, when this *status aparte* was officially confirmed by the Kingdom of the Netherlands.

Since then, Arubans have enjoyed extensive independence in determining the island's policies. According to the treaty, Aruba was to achieve complete independence by 1996; however, in March of 1994 it was agreed to postpone this status indefinitely.

The Yellow and the Black Gold

In 1816, Aruba was finally given back to the Dutch. Eight years later, the English probably regretted this because gold was discovered on Aruba's northern coast in 1824. The yield was somewhat more than 1,300 kilograms (1,085 pounds) of gold and then mining was discontinued in 1916. In the interim (1859), phosphate was also discovered and exported to the US and Europe. The search for gold had hardly been abandoned when black gold, namely oil, discovered Aruba: the Lago Oil Transport Company was impressed with Aruba's geographical location and political stability. The company built a port of transhipment for crude oil near San Nicolas. The harbour was extended and deepened for tankers and in 1929, an oil refinery began processing crude oil on Aruba.

Holidays and Celebrations

■ January 1: New Year's Day

As in many places throughout the world, the new year is welcomed with fireworks, music and dancing on Aruba. Of course, no one works on New Year's Day with only the fewest exceptions. On New Year's Eve, all the larger hotels present shows with dancing, folkloric performances and dinner. For these events, be sure to reserve tickets since the shows are often sold out days beforehand. Information can be found in the large advertisements in the free newspapers.

■ February: Carnival/Mardi Gras

On the weekend before lent begins on Ash Wednesday (40 days before Easter) a festive and vivacious atmosphere sweeps over Aruba; colourful costumes, often the result of a year's hard work, bands, dancing and parades shake the island. The *Lighting Parade* takes place on Sunday in Oranjestad, making for a spectacle in its own right. Monday is a day of recovery; the stores remain closed.

■ March 18: Anthem and Flag Day, national holiday

On March 18, 1976, Aruba's flag *(→ National Flag)* was hoisted for the first time. For this reason, the island's (relative) independence has been celebrated on this day for several years. Flag parades take place in Oranjestad and St. Nicolas, school children sing the national anthem and many, many Arubans celebrate this day on the beach with music, beer and a barbecue.

■ April: Easter

As in all Christian nations, the Easter holidays are important on Aruba. Stores remain closed. In 1997, Good Friday is on March 28th with Easter Sunday and Monday on March 30th and 31st.

■ April 30: Queen's Day

In the Netherlands, the queen's birthday is celebrated on April 30th; and the Arubans won't be left out. The agenda includes official celebrations as well

Quaint Dutch façades — the Dutch colonial period characterises Oranjestad even today

as musical parades and folkloric events. Of course, stores remain closed on this day.

■ **May 1: Labour Day**

This day in honour of work is celebrated by visiting the beach and relaxing.

■ **May 16: Christ's Ascension**

June — the "action month" on Aruba

The world's best **wind surfers** meet up on Aruba in the first weeks in June. The first week is reserved for amateurs; the second week marks the beginning of professional competition. Several thousands of dollars are at stake. Since the competitions can be seen so well from the beach, thousands upon thousands of surfing enthusiasts come to Aruba from the US and South America during these two weeks. Those who failed to book accommodation well in advance will have to sleep under the stars. Simultaneously, during the first two June weekends, the **Jazz & Latin Music Festival.** takes place on Aruba. In 1988, it was held for the first time. The month of June was chosen deliberately since this was the low season when relatively few tourists travelled to Aruba. This has changed drastically: jazz fans from around the world have meanwhile heard of the festival and many come to Aruba during the hot summer to enjoy — as was the case in 1993 — jazz greats like Patti Austin, Hiroshima, Jerry Rivera, Chris Walker, or Jon Secada.

■ **June 24: St. John's Day**

This day is celebrated heartily with the "burrying of the chicken" or in Papiamento: *"Derramento di Gai"*. In remembrance of the rooster that crowed three times in the passion in the Bible announcing the events that would come to pass, the rooster is buried on this day. Earlier a real rooster was put through this; today, a fake rooster is buried in the ground with only its head protruding. All those participating in the festivities are decorated in yellow or dressed completely in yellow and form a large circle around the rooster. The band place lively music and a dancer is blindfolded. Accompanied by music, the dancer then attempts to hit the rooster's head with a stick. All the children named Ian or John wear a dry cactus on their heads or at least carry one along. The cacluses are used to build a fire over which the dancers jump, accompanied by music.

■ **December 5: St. Nicholas' Day**

St. Nicholas is known throughout the world and Aruba is no exception. The good children are given presents and the naughty children are sent to Spain, so the legend goes. Already, days before December 5th, numerous St. Nicholas' can be seen roaming Aruba. They are usually accompanied by the figure "Black Peter" and hand out candy to the children. This is no easy job for a St. Nick considering he has to wear a heavy red cloak and a bushy beard in temperatures around 30°C (86°F) in the shade.

■ December 25 and 26: Christmas and Boxing Day

On Aruba, Christmas is celebrated somewhat differently. Children already receive their larger presents on St. Nicholas' Day. In those families which tend more towards the North American tradition, presents are exchanged on Christmas Day.

Insurance

During a trip to the Caribbean, it is best to be insured with **travel health insurance.** Usually, this type of policy costs only pennies per travel day. With it, visits to the doctor and medications are covered. Some policies include transport back home in emergencies. Price comparisons are worth the time. In normal cases, tourists must pay directly for treatment and medication to be reimbursed upon returning home. For this, receipts and invoices are needed.
Luggage insurance covers lost luggage — this has happened to tourists who travelled to Aruba via Caracas, and not rarely at that. Bags and suitcases can reach the wrong destination. Sometimes the luggage turns up later, sometimes it doesn't. Since the airlines only reimburse a fraction of the luggage's value, it is a good idea to take out luggage insurance and make a list of the luggage content.

International Press

Local **daily newspapers** (in Dutch) are *Diario* and *Bon Dia*. In addition, there are two other newspapers in Papiamento *(→ Language)*. More interesting for tourists: in the shops, supermarkets and hotels are free daily newspapers in English — *The News* and *Aruba Today,* financed through advertising. Both papers provide a brief overview of global events.
US daily newspapers and **magazines** are available in almost every larger hotel, but these are rather expensive.
Books: English paperbacks are available everywhere at high prices. They are usually three to four times as expensive as in the US.

Language

Visitors can experience a true linguistic wonder on Aruba. As so many aspects are such a colourful mix on this island, this is also true with the language. The official language on Aruba is Dutch and Dutch is spoken in the schools. However, local residents all speak *Papiamento*. This language is a mixture of Spanish, Dutch and Portuguese. In addition, words have been adopted from English and French and from native dialects. As an Aruban friend put it: *"It is the best language you can imagine. If you can't think of a word, then you just use one from another language."* Many of the local residents who immigrated to Aruba also speak Spanish and a large proportion of the population under-stands and speaks English. Thus, there will be no language problems on Aruba.

Another indication of the linguistic flexibility of local residents is a classified ad for a cashier, for example: "Willingness to work overtime expected. In addition, the applicant should speak Dutch, Papiamento English and Spanish."

Papiamento	English
Bonbini	Welcome (Hi)
Con ta bai?	How are you?
Mi ta bon.	I am fine.
Masha danki.	Thank you very much.
Bon dia/tardi/nochi	Good morning/evening/night.
Te aworo.	See you later.
Cuanto?	How much?

Leaving Aruba

Leaving the island from the *Reina Beatrix Airport* is just as simple as arriving on the island *(→ Travelling to Aruba)*. However, a departure tax of $12.50 (£7.50) or 22 florin per person must be paid, even if only leaving Aruba for a day trip to Bonaire or Curaçao.

Receipts for the tax paid are available at the colourful, hexagonal counter in the middle of the departures hall. This receipt is collected later with the return ticket, identification and a copy of the entry and exit form. The receipt and the copy of the form are kept by the officials. After this, the visitor has officially "left" the country.

The selections in the shops in the **duty-free** area is not overwhelming but it is possible to dispose of excess florins for a coffee, a soft drink or by purchasing souvenirs. After having passed through customs, the items purchased in a duty-free shop in the city are handed over. These items, whether duty-free cigarettes or even video recorders and cameras, are only delivered after passing through customs. With this, the government tries to prevent items purchased duty-free from being resold to local residents.

All **airlines** are represented by a handling agent in the departures hall. Be sure to reconfirm departures by telephone since flight schedules can change and it could happen that a departure is rescheduled earlier.

Airline or Handling Agent Telephone Numbers

Aeropostal, Tel: 31 892 or 39 040; **Air Aruba,** Tel: 23 151;**ALM,** Tel: 30 080; **American Airlines:** Tel: 23 777; **Avensa,** Tel: 27 779; **Avianca,** Tel: 23 388; **KLM,** Tel: 23 546 or 23 547; **Lufthansa / Condor,** Tel: 36 800; **Viasa,** Tel: 36 526

Maps

Those who would like to take a closer look at Aruba on a map at home can find detailed maps. Berndtson & Berndtson published a map with a scale of 1:50,000, available in good bookstores. On the reverse are maps of Oranjestad (scale 1:10,000), San Nicolas (scale: 1:20,000) and the beaches (scale 1:25,000). This map is entitled "Aruba Road Map" (ISBN 3-928855-00. Those who can wait will find more inexpensive maps on the island itself. Every bookstore and every service station on Aruba sell good maps priced around $1 (60p) or 1.75 florin. Even less expensive are the maps in the tourist information brochures. These are literally available on every street corner and are free of charge. These maps can be used in planning an island tour or a stroll through the shopping streets of Oranjestad. One small drawback: exact addresses of many restaurants and shops are not listed; merely the streets where they are located are included.

Medical Care

Numerous medical specialists trained in Europe and the US live in Aruba. There is hardly an island in the Caribbean with such high medical care standards than on the "island under the wind". And in the **Hospital Dr. Horacio Oduber,** the staff is competent and quick to help, whereby the first question does not concern insurance coverage. The invoice arrives afterwards, whether the patient was in the clinic or at the doctor.

The hospital lies between the two hotel chains "low rise hotels" and "high rise hotels" *(→ Accommodation).*

Important Telephone Numbers

Emergency: 115
General Practitioners: Boekhoudt, Tel: 31 612; Hagens, Tel: 45 073; Hernandez, Tel: 47 678; Ho Kang You, Tel: 21 880; Lacle, Tel: 24 416; Leo, Tel: 36 074; L'Isle, Tel: 23 412; Normann, Tel: 71 055; Romero, Tel: 28 239; Samuels, Tel: 45 347; Tiemessen, Tel: 73 100; Trikt, Tel: 34 500.
Specialists: *Surgeons:* Berlinski, Tel: 33 968; Engelbrecht, Tel: 76 842; Ho Kang You, Tel: 78 650; Saladin, Tel: 78 864.
Gynaecologists: Ho Kang You, Tel: 33 988; Lopez-Dorado, Tel: 78 910; Tijon Sie Fat, Tel: 34 713.
Internal Medicine: Anaya, Tel: 76 818; Essed, Tel: 76 701; Falconi, Tel: 75 034.
Paediatricians: Bryson, Tel: 78 875; Croes, Tel: 76 794.
Neurologist: Valleho, Lopez, Tel: 78 890.
Orthopaedic Surgeon: Windt, Tel: 75 070.
Urologist: Moreta, Tel: 64 334.

Money

Aruba's official **currency** is the Aruban florin (Afl). One hundred cents make up one florin. Practically everywhere, tourists can pay in US dollars, but there can be problems when paying with a $100 bill. Merchants are wary of counterfeit bank notes. The florin to dollar exchange rate is set: at banks, $1 is equal to 1.77 florin with cash and 1.78 florin with cheques. In shops, dollars are converted to 1.75 florin.
Items in shops are always priced in florin (Afl or fl) and usually in US dollars as well.
Credit Cards: VISA, American Express and Master Card (Eurocard) are accepted in almost every store, restaurant, and bar (with a minimum purchase limit). Important exceptions: supermarkets, fast food restaurants and ice cream parlours do not accept credit cards. Credit cars are recommended for renting cars or surfboards.
Some banks like Interbank and Amros Bank also accept **Eurocheques.** However, these must be issued in one's home currency. Regardless of the amount on the cheque (maximum of £160) the banks charge 2.50 florin as a commission. **Traveller's Cheques** in US dollars are also accepted in hotels and banks.

Mosquitoes

A strip of swamps or an area which stands under water during the rainy season extends behind the high and low rise hotels as well as behind the buildings in Malmok. This makes for an ideal breeding ground for mosquitoes. Their bites do not remain evident as long as those from their colleagues in North America but private homes and guest houses are equipped with screens on the windows.

Therefore, don't leave doors or windows without screens standing open. A mosquito net over the bed can prove helpful. There are also insect repellents available on Aruba, albeit at higher prices than at home.

Motorcycles and Mopeds

An alternative to a rental car is a rental motorcycle or moped; however, this is not necessarily a more economical option. Also, be sure to consider the wind and sand on the streets which can cause skids if the driver is not experienced with handling a motorcycle. In addition to this, most sights are accessible only over gravel roads with huge potholes, requiring the driver's undivided attention.

Renting a motorcycle or moped works exactly the same way as renting a car (→ *Car Rental*).

Here, too, be sure to call and ask for prices. If a motorcycle is then rented, the rental agency picks the renter up and brings him or her to the motorcycle. Of course, one or two helmets are included in the rental price.

A motorcycle with 95cc, appropriate for one person, usually costs $30 (£18) per day and $180 (£108) per week. A more powerful machine with 125cc, appropriate for two persons, costs $37 (£22) per day and $201 (£121) per week. A motorcycle with 200cc costs $40 (£24) per day and $216 (£130) per week. The most powerful motorcycle with 600cc costs $57 (£35) per day and $301 (£181) per week.

Rental Agencies

George's Cycles: Tel: 25 975 or 31 235; L. G. Smith Blvd. 135 (entrance to Oranjestad); **Hill Motor Rent,** Tel: 66 663 or 66 662; Noord 86 A; **Melchor Cycle Rental:** Tel: 23 448; Leendert 170 A; **Nelson Cycle Rental,** Tel: 66 801; Gasparito 10 A; **Palm Beach Motor,** Tel: 68 888; Noord 88 A; **Ron's Cycle Rental,** Tel: 62 090; Bakval 17 A; **Semver Cycle,** Tel: 66 851; Noord 22

Mountain Bikes

Despite the heat and dust, mountain bikes are becoming increasingly popular on Aruba. And to be sure: a tour by mountain bike in the early morning or shortly before sunset is a lot of fun on the rarely driven trails in the sparsely populated northeastern regions of the island. By no means should tourists cycle after dark. There are far too many speeding cars on the island which are hardly accustomed to cyclists in traffic *(→ Driving and Traffic Regulations)*. Avid cyclists will hardly be satisfied with the condition of rental mountain bikes (normal bicycles can hardly be recommended due to the dusty trails). Be happy if all fourteen gears and the breaks work. Be sure to have the handlebars and seat adjusted for you.

Those who are especially tall or short should mention this when ordering a bike. With growing competition, it can be hoped that the condition of the mountain bikes offered will improve.

One of the first rental agencies was *"Pablito's Bikes Rental"*, L. G. Smith Blvd. 228. This agency brings the bike or bikes to the hotel (Tel: 78 655 or 75 010). A mountain bike costs $45 (£27) per week.

Where to Rent Mountain Bikes

Corvalou offers guided mountain bike tours on Saturdays and Sundays, costing $15 (£9) per person. Of course, mountain bikes can be rented by the day or week as well. Tel: 35 742 or 30 487.

Also sharing in the mountain bike rental market are **Ron's Cycle Rental,** Tel: 62 090 and **Donata Cycle Rental,** Tel: 34 343 or 22 633.

National Flag

The Arubans are proud of their own flag, which emphasises the island's independence. The light blue background symbolises the never-ending sea, surrounding a red star symbolising the island. The star points in the four directions of the compass from which the island's residents once came and from which tourists now come. The star is bordered in white, similar to the white beaches which frame the island. Yellow it the colour of independence and the blossoming aloe.

Aruba's national flag was first hoisted on March 18,1976. This day *(Flag Day)* is now a national holiday, celebrated on Aruba's beaches, in Oranjestad and San Nicolas with parades, dancing and music.

Two days prior to this, on March 16, 1976, the Aruban song *"Aruba Dushi Tera"* (Aruba, beloved land) was declared the national anthem.

Aruba Dushi Tera	Aruba, beloved Land
Aruba patria apreciá *nos cuna venerá* *chicito y simpel bo por ta* *pero sí respetá*	Aruba, beloved homeland, safe cradle for us all. Although small and simple, we treasure you above all.
O, Aruba dushi tera *nos baranca tan stiná* *nos amor pa bo ta' sina grandi* *cu n'tin nada pa kibré* *Bo playanan tan admirá* *cu palma tur dorná* *bo escudo y bandera ta* *orguyo di nos tur*	O, Aruba, dear land, cliffs we love so dear, our love for you is so great that nothing can shake it. Your beaches, much admired, with palms richly adorned, your coat-of-arms, your flag are symbols for our pride.
Grandeza di po pueblo ta *su gran cordialidad* *cu Dios por guia y conservá* *su amor pa libertad.*	So gracious, are your people may God guide them and preserve their love of freedom.

Night Life

Bars

Bars and pubs are abundant on Aruba. Every hotel has a bar and there is also at least a beach bar on all of the larger hotel beaches. These are well frequented, especially during happy hour when all drinks are half price. This usually begins at 5 pm, sometimes lasting two hours.

On the other hand, there are not many bars on Aruba which are not associated with a hotel. For this reason, night life is pretty much confined to the resort areas, meaning restaurant, bar, discotheque, shows and → *casinos* are all under one roof. There is something for every taste and the tourists' money stays in the hotels. A pub called *"Cheers"* at the harbour entrance on the corner of the Port of Call Shopping Centre next to " Lover's Ice Cream" is especially lively. Also popular are the disco/pub called *"The Cellar"* on Klipstraat and *"Que Pasa"* on Schelpstraat, both in the centre of Oranjestad on Daniel Leo Plaza with the quaint Dutch houses. There is a good mix of locals and tourists in all three bars, where local bands often perform.

In contrast, *"Charlie's Bar"* in San Nicolas is completely dominated by tourists. It is located on Main Street and is connected with a true legend. Fifty years ago, this was a hot spot for workers in the refinery and sailors looking for action, all of whom left their traces. In 1987, Charly died at the age of 73 and up to his last living day, he stood behind the bar telling his guests stories from times gone by. Today, his son carries on the tradition. And since the local residents could by no means leave as much money in the pub as tourists, the legend has taken a sharp turn.

The 'in' pubs change as quickly as the seasonal guests. It is worthwhile to ask other tourists for their recommendations which is also true with restaurants.

Prices: A beer (imported directly from the Netherlands) starts around $2 (£1.20) and cocktails start around $4 (£2.40).

Shows

Every larger hotel has an evening show à la Las Vegas with dancers from Brazil, Venezuela and even Las Vegas itself. Singers, duos and bands perform, talent shows are held and almost every day, beautiful girls compete

Blue as the endless sea: Aruba's national flag

to see who is indeed the fairest one of all. The show are very good in part, especially those with dancers.

Discotheques
Full-blown discos are not to be found on Aruba. When the mood hits its peak, then the rafters shake at *"Que Pasa"* on Schelpstraat, although there is no real dance floor. The atmosphere is liveliest *"Cheers"* when local bands perform there.

For a long time, the inside tip has been the upper floor in *"The Cellar"* on Klipstraat in Oranjestad. On Wednesdays, Fridays and Saturdays, the metal door to the upper floor is opened, signalling the beginning of a lively evening. Not techno music but dancing is the atmosphere set by the DJs. The best part: to save the investment in an expensive air conditioning system, there is simply no roof — dancing under the stars at its best.

Nudism

There is no official nudist beach on Aruba. On the popular beaches along the hotels, women swimming or sunbathing topless is sooner the exception as well. The rule of thumb: on more crowded beaches, people will be offended by topless and even more so by bottomless swimmers or sunbathers. On the other side of the island, far away from the hotel beaches, swimming or sunbathing in the nude can hardly offend anyone since hardly anyone is there. Only a handful of surfers and couples come to this area. However, the beaches are left to "nature" meaning that no one removes the rubbish washed up on shore. And it is not uncommon that a rental jeep will speed by sunbathers churning up sand.
(→ *Beaches and Swimming*)

The People of Aruba

There are several good reasons to travel to Aruba for a holiday: the sea, the sun, the beaches... Another very good reason is Aruba's people. The island residents are widely known for their openness and hospitality towards visitors and locals alike. Around 78,000 people live on Aruba, a third of which were actually born on the island. The rest originate from other Caribbean islands. Visitors will not be confronted with racism or discrimination on Aruba. Over 40 nations are represented in Aruba's population and the people obviously live in harmony. One reason for this tolerance and the very low crime rate is most certainly the high standard of living — especially when compared to other Caribbean islands. And the high standard of living can in turn be attributed to the high level of education in the populace. Over 95% of the island's residents can read and write.

A few more statistics: The life expectancy of Aruba is 72 years on average and the average age of Aruba's residents is 32.7 (as of September 1993).

Aruba's original inhabitants were the Arawak Indians, living mainly from fishing and collecting shellfish. When the Spaniards discovered Aruba (as well as Bonaire and Curaçao), they forced the Arawaks to work in the South American gold mines. Later, if they survived, the Arawaks were allowed to return to the island. However, when the Dutch took over the island in 1636, many Arawaks fled to the nearby mainland. The Dutch did not really take much note of those Arawaks who stayed. For the most part, they left the Arawaks to themselves or to the Spanish missionaries.

Since agriculture was not possible on Aruba due to the → *climate,* the Dutch used the original inhabitants as goatherds or to tend a handful of cattle which roamed the island freely.

The dry climate also had an effect on the population's development. Since setting up plantations was not possible, no slaves were brought to Aruba. Thus, the Arawaks mixed with the Spanish and Dutch colonists over the years and not, as on Curaçao for example, with African slaves. Many of the island's residents of Arawak descent have a much lighter complexion than the residents on Aruba's sister islands.

Around 1800, Aruba's last Arawaks who still spoke their native language were buried. With this, the Arawaks lost an important component of their cultural identity.

At the beginning of the 20th century, with the discovery of oil in Venezuela and the construction of an oil refinery on Aruba, came numerous immigrants from other islands and nations. These immigrants quickly mixed in with the island's population.

Pharmacies

For tourists, the most easily accessible pharmacy lies directly next to the Dr. Horacio Oduber Hospital on L. G. Smith Blvd. near the "low rise hotels" (→ *Medical Care).* The pharmacy is housed in the "Eagle Medical Centre", where a number of specialists have their offices. On the roof is a large green sign with yellow lettering. On sale in the front area are a number of items which can be found in most drug stores, from suntan lotion to vitamin tablets to baby products. In the rear area of the store is the pharmacy with prescription and non-prescription medications

Medication prices are noticeably lower than in central Europe. All customers receive a receipt so they can be reimbursed by their health insurance company upon returning home.

The pharmacy is open from 7:30 am to 7:30 pm. The staff speaks English and the pharmacist also speaks German. Tel: 76 103 pr 79 011.

Other Pharmacies and Drug Stores in Oranjestad

Botica Del Pueblo, Caya G. F. Betico Croes 48, Tel: 22 154
Botica Kibrahacha, Havenstraat 30, Tel: 22 007
El Luvre, Gutenbergstraat 6, Tel: 34 109

Photography

Film with a low light sensitivity (100 ASA) is the best bet for Aruba since the sun is very intense. A UV-filter for the lens is also of advantage because this will bring out the colours. Without a UV-filter, the sky, for example, will appear grey and almost white in the pictures. for the evening — and the sun sets quite abruptly — a flash is important to have along.

Film can be found almost everywhere on Aruba. Every hotel shopping area will carry film and there are photo-shops on almost every street corner in Oranjestad which carry all types of film. Film is more expensive than at home and development and prints are very expensive. Twenty-four exposures cost around 25 florin ($16.50/£10) to have developed and 36 exposures, around 37 florin ($21.50/£13).

A new trend: snap the pictures, discard the camera

On Aruba, the *disposable camera* is pretty much everywhere. Priced around $20 (£12) are cameras with 24 and 36 exposures in all types of light sensitivity, even waterproof disposable cameras are now on the market. Although some will consider this wasteful, these cameras are ideal for taking pictures under water or when on board a ship. There is no risk of ruining an expensive camera with sea water. Here too: check

---

If the camera should break or a spare part is needed, there are several electronics shops on Oranjestad's main street which offer a good selection of lenses, cameras, flashes, etc. Prices are higher than at home for these items as well.

Aruba's hotels are inviting holiday oases surrounded by lush, tropical vegetation

Police

The Aruban police are in fact most noticeable in that they are hardly noticeable at all. The crime rate is very low. This speaks for the effectivity of the police. The police officers are generally friendly and willing to help in any way they can. On Aruba, there is also a *beach patrol*. The officers use a three-wheeled dune buggy of sorts with huge tires, something similar to a riding lawn mower, to patrol the beaches.

In addition, *private guards* patrol shopping centres, various shops like exclusive boutiques, jewellery stores and banks. They will also help in an emergency.

Emergencies: In cases where the help of the police is urgently needed, call 111 00. In other cases, contact the individual police stations.

Police Station Telephone Numbers

Oranjestad, Tel: 24 000, Wilhelminastraat 40
San Nicolas, Tel: 45 000, Bernhardstraat
Saveneta, Tel: 47 000
Noord, Tel: 78 000
Beach Patrol, Tel: 63 003 *(→ Emergencies)*

Politics

Aruba has a parliamentary democracy. The head of state is the queen of the Kingdom of the Netherlands. The queen is represented on the island through her governor, who is nominated by the Aruban government; the governor's term is six years. The prime minister heads a cabinet of six ministers, responsible for domestic policy, economy and tourism, justice, transport and communication, social and labour policy and public health. In the Hague, Netherlands, an additional minister represents Aruba's interests in the Dutch government as a member of the Council of Ministers.

The Aruban government owns some companies which are pivotal in providing for the needs of its citizens. Thus, the water and energy company *WEB,* the telephone company *SETAR* and the electricity company *ELMAR* are directly subject to governmental policy.

The cabinet must answer to the parliament, comprising one house. The 21 members of parliament are newly elected every four years.

At present, there are eight political parties on Aruba. Of these, five are represented in parliament. In addition, there are five different unions, several trade associations and even some clubs which are active in forming public opinion.

One of the most significant aspects of governmental activity is the social security of the population which has reached high standards on Aruba. For example, prices for food staples like sugar, milk, flour and rice are fixed by the government. Also, employees who earn less than around $19,000 (£11,400) a year must have his or her health and accident insurance provided by their employer. In addition, every Aruban over 62 is paid a pension; the premiums for this pension plan are paid by the government. The normal working time is 8½ hours a day with a maximum of 45 hours and six days per week. A week may have at most 48 hours of work.

Overtime must be paid with a supplement of at least 50%. In addition, employees must have 15 days of paid vacation.

An important basis for Aruba's future is its **education system:** Around 16% of the governmental budget is invested in Aruba's schools. Educational facilities range from kindergartens (45 kindergartens with around 2,000 children) to primary schools (32 schools with over 7,000 pupils) two special education schools for remedial education, secondary education schools (22 schools with around 5,000 pupils) three polytechnics schools for engineering, administration and commerce (especially hotel administration; 580 students) all the way to a small university which, however, offers education only in teaching and law. Illiteracy on Aruba is extremely low. Ninety-five percent of the population can read and write. The classroom language is Dutch even in primary education. In the secondary schools, English and Spanish are mandatory. There are no fees for attending school so almost all of Aruba's children do attend.

Postal System

The **main post office** is located on Boerhavestraat in Oranjestad. *Directions (on foot):* Take the Caya G. F. Croes (main shopping street) heading south out of town; turn left onto Hendrikstraat which then turns into Kerkstraat and Boerhavestraat. To the right is the Roman Catholic St. Franciscus Church. One hundred metres farther, on the left, is the large postal building with a parking area in the front. The post office is open Monday to Friday from 7:30 am to noon and from 1 to 4:30 pm. Postage stamps are available here. Letters and postcards can be deposited at any time outside the building to the far left when facing the building. In a side building to the right, it is also possible to send telegrams and faxes.

For guests of the high rise hotels and those coming from Malmok: At the entrance to the Holiday Inn (high rise hotels, L. G. Smith Blvd. 230) there is a bright red mailbox with no writing on it to the left of a column. Of course, hotel reception desks will also take letters and postcards.

With some luck, a letter can reach Europe within five days but they usually take ten to fourteen.

Stationery and *envelopes* can be found in the shopping centres. *Postcards* are available all over the city (four for $1/60p) even in the supermarkets. *Postage stamps* are also available in bookstores.

A post card to Europe costs 70 Aruban cents and an airmail letter to Europe, at least 1,50 florin. If sending packages, there are two options: either the post office or UPS at Italiestraat 3, Oranjestad, Tel: 357 14 or 356 83, Fax: 355 26.

Religion

Eighty to ninety percent of the Aruban population are Roman Catholic — somewhat surprising for a Dutch island. The Dutch settlers who then wanted to spur on their business interests on the island obviously had no interest in saving Indian souls. It was with all the more conviction that missionaries from Spain and Venezuela went to work: within a very short time, almost the entire native population had been baptised into the Catholic faith.

When the two big oil refineries were built, many immigrants came to the island, bring as many religions (→ *History*). Thus, Protestant and Catholic churches, Moslem mosques and Jewish synagogues can be found on Aruba. Visitors can call to find out information on church services.

Religious Congregations on Aruba

Apostaolic: Bernhardstraat 185, San Nicolas (Sundays at 10:30 am and 7:30 pm), Tel: 48 710

New Apostolic: Goletstraat 5A (Sundays at 9:30 am, Wednesdays at 7 pm), Tel: 33 762

Baptist: Bernhardstraat 18, San Nicolas, Tel: 48 179

Evangelical: Huygenstraat 17, Oranjestad (Sundays 9 am and 7 pm), Tel: 22 058

Jehova's Witnesses: Guyabastraat 3 (Tuesdays, Thursdays and Saturdays at 7:15 pm), Tel: 28 963

Jewish: Adrian Laclé Blvd., Oranjestad (Fridays at 8:00 pm), Tel: 23 272

Catholic: St. Anna Church, Noord (Sundays at 7:30 am and 6 pm), Tel: 21 409

Lutheran: Wilhelminaplein (Sundays at 10 am), Tel: 21 435

Restaurants

The number of restaurants on Aruba is overwhelming. Italian, Argentinean, German, Chinese, American; steaks, seafood, fast food: everything can be found on the island. Good and very expensive restaurants are just as much present as more reasonably priced eateries. And the only recommendation that can be trusted is to try as many as possible. What was a good recommendation last month can be quite the opposite now. Cooks are scarce, in great demand and change jobs frequently. Therefore, it is best to ask other tourists for their recommendations. Asking taxi drivers or hotel employees is not as good because they often receive a commission from restaurant owners if they send customers to their restaurants.

In almost all of the better restaurants, **reservations** are expected. Not that guests without reservations are turned away at the door, but depending on the restaurants' popularity and the season, they can fill up quickly. Without reservations, there could be a long wait. Another piece of advice: even at Pizza Hut, guests are seated by a host.

The menus: These are often in two, sometimes three languages, always including English. Quite often, there are lighted pictures of the food at the restaurant entrance. Good wines are available in all restaurants; often, these come from California, Chile, France and sometimes Germany.

The following restaurants have a good reputation:

■ Brisas del Mar

Savaneta 222, head towards San Nicolas then follow the signs, Tel: 47 718. The restaurant is situated sea side and opens to the Caribbean. Numerous ceiling fans make for a pleasant breeze. Through a window, guests can watch the cooks at work. The seafood, the restaurant's speciality, is very good. The service is very friendly. The restaurant is open for lunch from noon to 3 pm except Mondays and for dinner from 6:30 to 10 pm. Medium price range

■ Driftwood

Klipstraat 12, Tel: 32 515. The restaurant lies in the middle of Oranjestad near the central plaza. The walls are covered with driftwood with a decor of ship lanterns and huge ropes on the walls and bar. In this very popular restaurant (be sure to make reservations), there is a lot of bustling activity. The fish dishes are good. According to the advertising, the boss catches the fish himself. It is also possible to go on a fishing trip aboard the restaurant's own fishing boat 'Driftwood'. Medium price range

■ Waterfront Crabhouse

In the Harbourtown Market on the yacht harbour in Oranjestad. The restaurant, like its neighbour "Waterfront", lies at the end of the shopping market. Both restaurants have a large terrace where guests can dine and enjoy the sunset. Like the name says, the Crabhouse has specialised in crab and lobster which can be seen in the large aquarium. Reservations are not necessarily a must. Higher price range

■ Waterfront

The "Waterfront" is right next door to the "Crabhouse" on Oranjestad's yacht harbour, Tel: 36 767. The food served is highly diverse, ranging from burgers and fries to steaks all the way to seafood. Reservations are not a must here. No credit cards accepted. Medium price range

Other restaurant worth recommending:

■ Bon Appetit

Palm Beach 29, Tel: 65 241. The lettering on the sign already shows that the food is hearty here — like at a ranch. Despite this, there is seafood on the menu. The restaurant is open from 5 to 11 pm, closed Sundays. Higher price range

■ Boonoonoonoos

Wilhelmstraat 18a, Tel: 31 888. The restaurant with the funny name sees itself as an authentic eatery with Aruban and French cuisine. Fish dishes are emphasised. The restaurant is open from 5 to 11 pm. Higher price range

■ La Bouillabaisse

Bubali 69, Tel: 71 408. The owner is French and travelled through the world as a cook before coming to Aruba. After having worked in a number of Aruban restaurants, he opened his own. Fish dominates the menu here as well. The restaurant is open from 6 to 11 pm, closed Tuesdays. Higher price range

■ Buccaneer

Gasparito Road 11C in Noord, Tel: 66 172. One part of the decor is in the form of a sunken sailing ship. In the 12 potholes are fish in a saltwater aquarium. The other room looks like an underwater cave and a huge aquarium completes the aquatic motif. The two managers serve the guests themselves. The speciality is fish. The Buccaneer is open from 6 to 11 pm, closed Sundays. Higher price range

■ Chez Mathilde

Havenstraat 23, Tel: 34 968. The doorman in his white uniform is already an indication: this is not a restaurant where you pop in for a quick bite to eat. Guests visit "Mathilde" only in proper attire and usually with a wad of money. The building is over one hundred years old and was named after the last owner. The restaurant specialises in fish and seafood. The meat served comes only from cattle which grazed on special pastures. The restaurant is open from 11:30 am to 2:30 pm for lunch (except Sundays) and 6 to 11 pm for dinner. Highest price range

■ El Gaucho

Wilhelminastraat 80, Tel: 23 677. The Gauchos have been in business over 15 years in their restaurant, specialising in Argentinean cuisine. Of course, there is also fish on the menu. All of the dishes are charcoal broiled. El Gaucho is open from 6 top 11 pm, closed Wednesdays. Higher price range

■ Gasparito

Gasparito 3, Tel: 67 044. The restaurant where Aruban artists also display their work serves Aruban and traditional cuisine. The pictures are for sale. Gasparito is open from 5 to 11 pm, closed Wednesdays. Higher price range

■ L'Escale Restaurant

Seaport Village in the business centre of Oranjestad, Tel: 36 000. The owner is French and the French influence is very apparent on the menu. It would be inappropriate to come here in shorts and a T-shirt. L'Escale Restaurant is open from 6:30 to 11 pm. Highest price range

■ Mama Mia

L. G. Smith Blvd., right across the street from the Sonesta Hotel in Oranjestad, Tel: 36 246. As one might guess from the name, this restaurant predominantly serves Italian cuisine but there is also seafood on the menu. "Mama" is very lively, guests are all more or less seated outside on the covered terrace overlooking the yacht harbour. The menu is displayed outside the entrance in the form of pictures with prices. Mama Mia also serves breakfast. The restaurant is open from 11 am to 11 pm. Higher price range

■ Papiamento Restaurant

Washington 61, Noord, Tel: 64 544. "International cuisine and grill" is on the first page of the menu. The menu includes foremost seafood like lobster and prawns but also steaks, lamb cutlets and chicken. Guests are seated either in the old, 'authentic' house from the 18th century or outside on the terrace, surrounding the pool. The Papiamento Restaurant is open from 6 to 11 pm. Higher price range.

■ Pavarotti

Palm Beach 21a, Tel: 60 644. What can be expected from a restaurant called 'Pavarotti'? Exactly, an Italian restaurant, but it also serves Argentinean steaks. What also sets this restaurant apart is it's large salad bar. Pavarotti is open from 6 to 10 pm. Higher price range.

■ Pirate's Nest
L. G. Smith Blvd. at the Best Western Manchebo Beach Resort, Tel: 31 100. The restaurant looks like a ship but is built of stone. Steaks and seafood dominate the menu but guests can also eat breakfast here, either on board or in front of the stone ship with a beautiful view of the sea. Open 7 am to 10:30 pm. Higher price range

■ Que Pasa?
Schelpstraat20 in Oranjestad, Tel: 26 490. "What's up?" is the restaurant's name. Actually, there is always something going on here and this restaurant isn't actually a restaurant at all. It is sooner a pub which also serves food. The portions here are large and comparatively reasonably priced. The menu changes almost daily and is sooner European/Dutch in character. Most guests come for the food and then the after dinner attractions: after 10 or 11 pm, the pub is hopping well into the wee hours of the morning. Open 6 pm to 4 am. Medium price range

■ Rigoletto
Bubali 16, Tel: 23 170. Opera echoes through the restaurant, lending it Italian flair. A peek into the menu reveals spaghetti Mafia, rigatoni... among the pasta dishes are also seafood dishes. Open from 6 to 11 pm, closed Mondays. Medium price range

■ The Flame
Noord 19a, Tel: 64 688. The restaurant can get a bit warm because the food here is prepared and flambéd tableside. The cuisine is international. "Steaks served with a flare" is the restaurant's slogan. Open 6 to 11 pm, closed Wednesdays. Higher price category

■ The Old Cunucu House
Palm Beach 150, Tel: 61 666. The small house in typically Aruban style is around 70 years old and was recently renovated. "Cunucu" is the name of the rural region in the island's interior. The restaurant specialises in typically Aruban cuisine. International cuisine is also served. The bar opens at 5 pm and the restaurant is open from 6 to 11 pm with live music on Fridays and Saturdays. Higher price range

■ The Steamboat Buffet
L. G. Smith Blvd. 370, Tel: 36 700. The "Steamboat" does not have the most refined atmosphere, but it does have reasonable prices. Popular with young and old, the atmosphere is often bustling. Breakfast and lunch are served for

International fast food: the most famous hamburger in the world can also be found on Aruba, but Aruba's cuisine has much more to offer

set prices and are "all you can eat". In the evening, there is à la carte service. Open 24 hours a day, this restaurant never closes. Low price range

■ Twinklebone's

Turibana Plaza, Noord, Tel: 69 806. Guests in this restaurant could very well encounter a singing cook or a dancing waiter. Steaks and seafood dominate the menu. Two live shows offer entertainment or annoyance (depending on one's taste) every evening. Open 6 to 10 pm, closed Sundays. Higher price range

■ Villa Germania

Harbourtown Market, directly on Oranjestad's yacht harbour, Tel: 36 161. Those with a craving for hearty German food will find friendly service as well at this restaurant. From the ever-popular *Apfelstrudel* to *Wiener Schnitzel* and even spaghetti Bolognese can be found on the menu. Breakfast is also served in the small restaurant. The owner of the "Villa" is a windsurfer and Austrian. Open 8 am to 10 pm. Medium price range

---

Eating Out — but not in restaurants

Every **bar** has snacks available. Another tip: two **white trucks** can be found on L. G. Smith Blvd. along the harbour during the evening. One is in front of the Harbourtown Market right in front of the Villa Germania Restaurant, the other is right next door to Domino's Pizza at the Schooner Market. These offer a variety of snacks from chicken to hot dogs served with pastechi, empanada and cala — highly recommended.

Shopping

Generally, everything necessary and not so necessary is available on Aruba. In addition to the small *shopping malls* in or near the larger hotels, there are five ***shopping centres*** competing for customers: first, the shopping centre at the northern entrance to Oranjestad near the two large supermarkets "Ling & Sons" and "Pueblo". Established and well frequented are the three shopping centres surrounding Oranjestad's harbour, the "Port of Call", the "Seaport Village Mall" and the "Harbour Market".

Most local residents and many tourists shop in Oranjestad's main shopping street, the *Caya Betivos Croes Straat*. Here, shoppers can find typical department stores in addition to the shops catering to tourists. This street can get quite crowded, but is definitely worth a visit. The selection is very broad, but is more or less tailored to the tastes of North American tourists. Thus,

"Birkenstock" shoes are very popular in the shoe stores catering to tourists. Another example are shops specialising in ceramic figures and porcelain from Germany and Switzerland. Especially common in Oranjestad are elegant jewellery shops with the finest of rings, necklaces and watches — with prices to match

Bargain Hunting

A less pleasant surprise: with only a few exceptions, items on Aruba are more expensive than in Europe and North America. Even with duty-free items, shoppers should be cautious. Be sure to check prices at home to ensure that those sale items are not actually more expensive. This is especially true for the shops selling video equipment, cameras and stereo equipment.

One of the few exceptions are "Clinique" cosmetics. These fine products cost around half the price charged in Europe.

Business Hours: Most stores, whether typical tourist shops or department stores, open for business around 10 am and close at 6 pm. They remain closed on Sundays with the exception of souvenir shops in the shopping centres around the harbour if a passenger ship docks. This is almost a certainty on Sundays. All of the stores on Aruba are equipped with **air conditioning.** When shopping, this means a repeated change from tropical heat to artificially cool air and back. Therefore, it can be a good idea to take along a sweatshirt or light vest to wear in the shops.

Typical Souvenirs

T-shirts, T-shirts and more T-shirts: in every colour and form, these are on sale everywhere in Aruba. Four T-shirts for $10 (£6) — the quality matches the price.

In various souvenir shops in the shopping areas, tourists will repeatedly find the same items: of course T-shirts, small wood carvings like "typical buses", boots, parrots and mobiles (mostly made in the Dominican Republic) and large wood carvings like cactuses.

Souvenirs which are actually produced in Aruba can be found at "Artesenia" in a small house next to the Aruba Tourism Authority's main office on L. G. Smith Blvd. at the northern entrance to Oranjestad. The pottery (vases and bowls), the pictures and knitted goods on sale here, however, will probably not evoke too much enthusiasm.

Sights

■ Alto Vista

The Spanish missionary *Domingo Antonio Silvester* had the Indians build a small church in the island's northeastern region around 1750. When no more residents settled into this area, the wooden church gradually fell into decay until a small Madonna chapel was built on the same site in 1952 in comme-moration of the original building. The Spanish crucifix is especially beautiful and this stood in the original church. A procession in honour of the Virgin Mary takes place in October. For this reason, white crosses line the winding roadway to Alto Vista. The chapel is always open; to Arubans, it is a symbol of peace on the island. In front of the church, two dogs 'happily' await visitors. Their names are "Happy" and "Happiness".

■ Andicuri

A private coconut plantation extends somewhat south of the coastal area with the → *Natural Bridge.* There is a wonderful view from the nearby hills.

■ Archaeological Museum

In the archaeological museum in Oranjestad, Zoutmanstraat, Tel: 28 979 are finds from archaeological digs. The pottery, tools, objects of art and skeletons tell the story of the island and the Indians who once inhabited it. The museum is open Monday to Friday from 7:30 am to noon and 1 to 2:30 pm.

■ Arikok National Park

The Arikok National Park extends between the eastern coast and Arikok Hill (188 metres/614 feet only one metre shy of the island's 'highest' mountain, the Jamanota). During a walk along the trails through this park, visitors can make the acquaintance of the island's flora and fauna. Indigenous trees like the Watapana (divi divi tree), Brazil trees and guayak trees line the trails. Among the trees and cactuses lie bizarre stone blocks; the origin of these remains a mystery. This beautiful, somewhat surreal landscape is at its best in the light of the morning or evening sun. The park is well signposted.

■ Ayo and Casibari

If a giant were to have played with huge stone and then simply left them strewn about, then this is how the rock formations of Casibari, or farther north with even larger rocks near Ayo, look. Huge diorite blocks make an inviting place to rock climb. Some of these blocks have been so heavily eroded that they have been hollowed out in places making it possible to hike through them.

The island's largest rock formation near Ayo is about as high as a house. A pathway leads to a hollow in which the island's most famous Indian rock drawing can be seen — a picture of a giant bird.

■ Balashi

On Aruba, even relatively insignificant areas have been deemed 'sights' or at least 'points of interest'. One example is Balashi, the gold smelting plant from the previous century near Spaans Lagoen (Spanish Lagoon). There is actually hardly anything to see here, only some remnants of walls and the remains of smelting pots and ovens. However, the story behind Balashi is interesting: in 1899, the Aruba Gold Concessions Ltd. received permission to build a gold smelting plant on this site. However, it took several years until it began operation. Investors were probably quite distraught because the investments were far higher than the actual profits from the gold. Six smelting ovens were built and the ore was transported by rail out of the mine. The smelting plant even had its own electrical supply which was the most modern in the world at that time. Because of the high costs and paltry profits, the management wanted to rid itself of the smelting plant as quickly as possible. They sold the

One special attraction is anchored in Oranjestad's harbour: a pirate ship

entire facility to the Aruba Gould Maatschappij. However, this company would not be happy with the smelting plant either. Operation was stopped in 1916.

■ Boca Prins

Aruba's eastern coast is steep and rugged. With massive cliffs, the island counters the waves driven against this side of the island by the winds. A beautiful area here is Boca Prins or "Dragon Mouth" in English, near California Point and the Fontein Cave. There, the waves have succeeded in carving a large bay out of the coastal cliffs. Huge waves run into the 'dragon's mouth' unobstructed. To the left and right, they crash against the cliffs — a fantastic view when seen from above. Swimming here is extremely dangerous and could prove fatal due to the tricky currents.

When looking inland, another beautiful view unfolds. From the coastline, white dunes can be seen. These seem unreal as they rise from the dark, barren landscape. The same phenomenon can be observed again at the → *California Lighthouse*.

■ Bushiribana

Massive blocks of stone remain of the Bushiribana facility, the gold smelting plant of Aruba Island Gold Mining Company one of the first on Aruba. It was built in 1872. However, only ten years was the "Pirate's Fortress" in operation. Then it was shut down due to lack of profits — the surrounding area is scattered with mine shafts. Warning signs posted on cactuses advise caution in exploring the area. No accidents with the abandoned mine shafts have occurred to present. From Bushiribana, there is a lovely view of the barren landscapes of the eastern coast.

■ California Lighthouse

This is *the* point of orientation on the island and it remains an important point of orientation out at sea — the California Lighthouse. Amid the lunar landscape of Aruba's northern point, which has lost much of its original character through the construction of the Tierra del Sol Golf Course, the white lighthouse towers into the sky. It offers a wonderful view of the sea. Observing a sunset from the lighthouse is especially worthwhile. On a clear evening, it is possible to see Columbia. The slowly decaying house 30 metres away with its beautiful terrace was once a restaurant. Despite all the efforts by the owner and the island's government, the restaurant went bankrupt because taxi drivers refused to drive guests over the 300 metres of dirt roadway which made the taxis dusty. Now, the restaurant will be integrated into the golf course project.

■ Caves

"Tunnel of Love", "Huliba", "Guadirikiri", "Fontein" — so are the melodious names of the caves which can be found on Aruba's western coast and are among the island's attractions.

The **Tunnel of Love** is around 200 metres (220 yards) long and the ceiling is 5 to 6 metres (16 to 20 feet) high. A guide accompanies visitors through the system of caves for a small fee. He also recounts the love story behind the Tunnel of Love. The Huliba Caves also belong to the Tunnel of Love complex. These are two large chambers at a depth of around 30 metres (98 feet) connected by a corridor.

The **Guadirikiri Caves** are not as gloomy as for example the Huliba. Skylights to the earth's surface allow light into the caves with ceilings as high as 7 metres (23 feet). In darker areas, bats hang from the ceiling. Don't believe it if told the rock drawings are authentic, they aren't. These were painted on the cave's walls for a film and were never removed. The caves are around 150 metres (164 yards) long.

The **Fontein Caves** are Aruba's most beautiful. Fantastic Indian rock drawings embellish the cave's ceiling — and these *are* authentic. The main chamber around 30 metres long and about 12 metres wide (98 by 33 feet) is full of stalactites and stalagmites (whereby stalagmites go from the ground up and stalactites hang from the ceiling). The Fontein cave system is almost 100 metres (110 yards) long.

■ Coin Museum

In the *Numismatic Museum,* over 30,000 coins and bank notes from over 100 nations are on display. The museum is located on J. E. Irausquinplein in Oranjestad, a bit farther east from Fort Zoutman. The Numismatic Museum is open Monday to Friday from 9 to noon and 2 to 5 pm, Saturday from 10 am to noon and 2 to 5 pm.

■ Costal Oil Refinery

In 1929, the Lago Oil and Transport Company built a large refinery on Aruba's southwestern point. It became the largest in the world — up to eight thousand people found work in the refinery and many came to Aruba from other Caribbean islands for this very reason. The company chose Aruba for the location of its refinery because of its political stability and proximity to the oil fields of Lake Maracaibo in Venezuela. Daily, 440,000 barrels of oil were processed (one barrel is 158.97 litres or 42 gallons). Huge tankers brought the oil and picked it up again; the harbour was expanded to accommodate the tankers. However, in 1985, the refinery was closed due to overproduction. This was the stimulus for the government to look for a new source of income — and tourism was discovered. In 1990, the refinery was reopened by the

Coastal Corporation of Texas. It is planned to process only 150,000 barrels of oil per day.

In the refinery's golden days, when money could be made quickly, the American company built their skilled workers and managers a small city of their own. There, the high-paid employees could enjoy western comforts with their families (→ *Seroe Colorado*).

■ Cunucu

Cunucu is the term for the inland portion of Aruba where farming and raising cattle is still practised. The fields are often fenced in with cactuses. Cunucu, however, is also a term for small houses which the residents with relatively high standards of living can afford.

■ De Palm Island

As mentioned in the section on → *Excursions,* the De Palm travel organisation (Tel: 24 400) has secured many rights and opportunities to offer tourists diverse recreational activities. The selection includes the small De Palm Island off Aruba's southwestern coast with its fantastic beaches. Of course, there are all the facilities tourists could want here, like bars, restaurants etc. (Tel: 24 799). Even snorkellers will find ideal diving areas on "Palm Island".

■ Divi Divi

Under the entry → *Vegetation,* this tree was already mentioned, but deserves mention as a characteristic sight on the island: the divi divi tree. In Papiamento (→ *Language),* this indigenous tree is also called Watapana. Visitors will notice the tree which grows predominantly in the → *Arikok National Park* by its characteristic form — its crown grows in the direction of the wind. Thus, on Aruba with its constant westerly wind, the tree grows eastward. The divi divi blossoms are yellow, almost white, and have an intense aroma. The divi divi is a symbol of Aruba.

■ Fisherman's Hut

Somewhat north of the "high rise hotels" lies the beach that is especially well known among windsurfers: Fisherman's Hut. At this beach, no hotels, buildings or hills obstruct the wind. It blows with undaunted speed, even spurred on by air heating up over the island, blowing over Fisherman's Hut Beach and then out over the turquoise sea. A paradise for windsurfers. The anchored

The California Lighthouse: the main point of orientation on Aruba

fishing boats are picturesque with the colourful windsurfing sails flitting over the water.

■ Fort Zoutman

Fort Zoutman, the oldest building on the island, decided Aruba's fate twice: in 1796, the fort was built on the Paardenbaai to protect the harbour. The fort's four cannons were used only twice in Aruba's history, once by the Dutch themselves. But one thing at a time: In 1799, the Dutch were at war with England when the English ship "Hermione" appeared off Aruba's coast, the crew intent on conquering the island. With a few well-placed shots from Fort Zoutman's cannons, however, the English were forced to retreat. A few years later, Aruba would fall under English rule. And six years after the first shots were fired at the English ship, the English used the same cannons to shoot at the Dutch approaching the island once more. In 1816, Aruba was once again Dutch.

In 1868, the tower on which Aruba's first public clock was installed and which also served as a lighthouse, was added to the fortress. At night, lanterns were hung on the tower to warn approaching ships. Lanterns were lit for the first time on the Dutch King Willem III's birthday; thus, the tower's name. Today, the fort houses the Museo Historico Arubano (→ *Historical Museum*).

■ Historical Museum

The Museo Historico Arubano is housed in → *Fort Zoutman* on Zoutmanstraat in Oranjestad. On display are shards of pottery, stones, fossils, seashells and tools for processing gold and aloe. The historical museum offers a good overview of Aruba's turbulent history. The museum is open Monday to Friday from 9 am to noon and 1 to 4:30 pm.

■ Hooiberg / Hay Mountain

It is just 170 metres (546 feet) high, and with this, 20 metres (65 feet) short of the two 'highest' mountains on the island. However the Hooiberg (Hay Mountain) is immediately apparent from its volcanic cone shape. No wonder the Arubans view this along with the → *divi divi tree* as one of the island's symbols. On the Hooiberg, the effect of the wind on the vegetation is apparent. On its western slope facing the winds, vegetation is rather sparse while on the leeside to the east, cactuses and divi divi trees are denser. The Hooiberg's summit offers a panorama of the island, giving an impression of just how tiny Aruba actually is. The Hooiberg can be climbed over numerous steps, but this requires good physical condition.

■ Jamanota

All those who think the → *Hooiberg* is too small or difficult to climb, can try the Jamanota. The summit at 189 metres (618 feet) is Aruba's highest 'mountain' and is easily accessible by car. The Jamanota also offers a view over the entire island.

Natural Bridge

"The Natural Bridge — the largest and most impressive coral structure in the Caribbean." With these impressive words, this natural bridge is praised all over the island and indeed, the structure formed by the wind and waves from coral limestone is truly impressive — at least on postcards. In reality, it looks different: those who, after hearing the slogans and seeing the postcards, expect to see a huge natural bridge will be somewhat disappointed. In reality, the bridge is smaller than would be expected.

Olde Molen

Driving on the 1A motorway heading north, passengers will suddenly stare in astonishment. Yes, in the middle of the Caribbean landscape near the high rise hotels is indeed an authentic Dutch windmill. Even more strange is the fact that the windmill is near the bird sanctuary with swamps and cranes. It could truly be somewhere in the Netherlands. In 1962, tied to their traditions, the Dutch transported this windmill from 1815 to Aruba after dismantling it piece by piece to be rebuilt on the island. Today, the windmill houses a restaurant — with Delft tiles and paintings by the old Dutch masters.

Prison

On only the fewest maps is it mentioned and there are no official signs for it: Aruba's prison. It is quite a sight. Situated on the island's southeastern coast near the golf course and not far from the ghost town of → *Seroe Colorado,* the square building was placed on the cliffs with the wind and the high waves crashing against the coast. The prison stands like a defiant fortress against this backdrop. Of course, the prison cannot be toured. The prison has 280 sells and most of the inmates are small-time criminals. Severe crime is as good as non-existent. Jokesters claim that those prisoners with the longest sentences are given the cells with a view of the sea.

Salt Gardens

Earlier, salt was as valuable as gold; one reason for the Dutch to cross the ocean to conquer islands and nations and secure trading posts. For this reason, they were interested in Curaçao and Bonaire since the Spanish refused to provide them with any salt for picking herring. And since Aruba was not far, the island was quickly annexed. Later, salt was produced on Aruba as well. Near Saveneta and Palm Beach are remnants of these salt gardens. Today, they are used by numerous birds to nest.

Santa Anna

The Catholic Santa Anna Church in Noord was built in 1776 when the inhabitants were afraid to go to → *Alto Vista* because of a plague. Afterwards, it was renovated twice in 1831 and 1886 and its present-day appearance dates back to 1916. The church is renowned for its oak altar, a very good example of neo-Gothic art. The artist *Hendrik van der Geld* carved ten years on the altar before this work of art was presented to the Vatican at an exhibition in 1870. In 1928, the congregation of St. Anthony in Scheeveningen gave the majestic altar to the congregation of Noord. Santa Anna is very popular for weddings. The adjacent cemetery is also worth seeing.

■ Seroe Colorado

Aruba has everything it could need for a western film: like landscapes from the Wild West and it even has a ghost town.

When the Lago Oil Company built their refinery in the southeast near San Nicolas, the company needed the appropriate managers which were not to be found on the island. They needed to convince Americans to come to Aruba. In addition to a good salary, this was accomplished by building a small settlement with high living standards, Seroe Colorado. Elegant bungalows with swimming pools, its own church, a country club with tennis courts etc. made life comfortable for its residents. When business took a downward turn and ultimately forced the oil refinery to close (at present, it is operating on a skeleton crew) the Americans returned home. Seroe Colorado was abandoned and has been decaying since then.

■ Shipwreck

On May 10, 1940, the crew of the 130 metre (425 foot) German freighter "Antilla" sank their ship off the northern Aruban coast. The wreck lies at a depth of around 20 metres (65 feet), some parts protrude from the water. Today, the "German wreck" is a popular destination for excursion boats, scuba divers and snorkellers.

Sports and Recreation

Bowling

The Eagle Bowling Palace offers 12 lanes. The pink, fully air conditioned building also has a snack bar and a bar. It is open daily from 10 am to 2 am. From 10 am to 3 pm, an hour of bowling costs $10.50 (£6.30) or 18 florin and a 3 pm, the price increases to $11.50 (£6.90) or 20 florin. During the evening, the bowling centre fills quickly, making it a good idea to reserve a lane in advance by contacting Tel: 35 501 or 35 038.

> *Directions:* Eagle Bowling Palace is easily seen when heading north on the two-lane 1A roadway to California Lighthouse on the right between Pizza Hut and Taco Bell. Those driving from the north must turn left at the Royal Cabana Casino.

Golf

Unbelievable but true: Aruba will soon have the most beautiful golf course in the Caribbean — and this on an island with a climate that prohibits even a single blade of grass from growing. After 25 years of planning, the project directors are getting down to the nitty-gritty: since 1993, the graters and earth-moving equipment have been working in the middle of the lunar landscape on the multi-million dollar *Tierra del Sol* golf course .

In the arid landscape, where up to now only boats grazed and in which the lighthouse and an abandoned restaurant were the only noticeable signs of civilisation, grass now grows and excavators continue to churn up the earth. A series of small bungalows, villas and hotel complexes will be built here; in addition to this, a huge clubhouse with a restaurant, tennis courts and a swimming pool. The Tierra del Sol is scheduled to be completed very soon and open to visitors from around the world.

Deep-Sea Fishing

The owners of several boats anchored in Oranjestad's harbour are happy to rent out their boats for deep-sea fishing tours. This is by no means cheap; chartering a boat with a powerful motor and the appropriate fishing gear costs at least $350 (£210) for a full day.

Jetski

They're about as noisy as a motorcycle and by no means do they contribute to peace and tranquillity on the beach. What is terrible is when the jetskiers try to show off by jetting past swimmers and surfers barely missing them. This is why jetskiiers are meanwhile only allowed in certain zones. Jetskis can be rented almost everywhere near the larger hotels, diagonally across from the Amsterdam Manor Hotel. The last building in the "low rise hotel" row on Palm Beach is even a rental centre for these aquatic motorcycles. One half hour on a one-seater costs $35 (£21) and a two-seater, $55 (£33). These prices are not subject to bargaining; renters could have some luck negotiating more time for the same price.

Miniature Golf — and more

Next to the 1A motorway, shortly beyond Taco Bell, a hill rises from the landscape covered with palms and lighted signs. In the evening, this area is immersed in bright light; this is "Joe Mendez Adventure Golf". Amid the greenery, waterfalls and a stream with rapids, visitors can play 18 holes of miniature golf and zip about in *paddleboats* or *bumperboats*. The bumperboats are the aquatic version of bumpercars. Paddleboats are used to conquer the rapids in the stream. Of course there is also food and drink available. The adventure golf course is open daily from noon to midnight. One round of golf costs $6.50 (£3.90); a round by paddleboat or bumperboat costs $5 (£3.90), Tel: 76 625.

Snorkelling

The clear, shimmering turquoise water along Aruba's beaches makes for a perfect place to go snorkelling. There are three areas where the snorkelling is especially worthwhile, two are accessible by land.

■ The first area lies directly on the beach on the 1A towards the California Lighthouse. Around 250 metres (275 yards) north of Roger's Windsurf Place at Fisherman's Hut (a flag marks Roger's Place), the otherwise flat sand beaches of the western coast are interrupted by a coral formation. The water has hollowed out an area under the coral. In the calm, deep waters, divers can observe numerous aquatic contemporaries up close.

■ The second area lies another 500 metres ($\frac{1}{3}$ mile) north. Follow the road to California Lighthouse (turn left at the sharp right curve, otherwise the road leaves the coast and heads inland). Around 250 metres (275 yards) farther, take another left onto a road which leads down to the sea. On the curve below are a few parking places; to the left, a footpath leads down to a small beach which is usually deserted during the week. Here, at the rock formations is a wonderful snorkelling area. During the day, a number of excursion boats owned by various organisers come by here and tie up to a buoy. The fish have grown accustomed to these visitors and wait to be fed. With a few bread crumbs, thousands of little friends can be made — they eat right out of your hand.

■ The third area, probably the most beautiful for snorkelling, lies exactly in this area, but 300 metres (327 yards) out to sea — it is the wreck of the German freighter which lies only metres under the water's surface and some portions still protrude. This is also the destination for several excursion boats starting from the large hotels. Very good swimmers can also swim out to the shipwreck from the beach. The Wreck of the "Antilla" with its mast and other taller parts sticking out of the water, is easily seen in the clear water. And a visit below the water's surface will bring the diver right into an adventure film.

Sailing

At the large watersports organisers *Pelican Watersports,* Tel: 31 228, 24 739 or 29 134, *Red Sails Watersport,* Tel: 31 603, and at *De Palm Tours,* Tel: 24 400 (all have so much advertising that they are difficult to miss) sailing tours lasting one hour to a full day can be booked.

Boats offered are old wooden ships, modern sailing vessels, catamarans and trimarans. The vessels are in good condition without exception. From the huge selection, one can choose, for example, "Sailing at Sunset", "Dancing to Disco on a Pirate Ship" or "Sailing into the Night". Prices start at $25 (£15) for a two-hour group tour and go all the way to $500 (£300) to charter a ship for one day.

Sailcarting

Sailcarting (like go-carting with a sail) is not done directly on the beach, but a few hundred metres inland: in a small three-wheeled vehicle with a seat powered by its sail, the driver is propelled up to 50 kph (30 mph). *Aruba Sailcart N.V.,* is open daily from 11 am to 6 pm. One half hour in a one-seater sailcart costs $15 (£9); for a two-seater, $20 (£12).

The restaurant and small bar operated by Aruba Sailcart N.V. offer refreshment afterwards. It is possible to reserve a cart in advance by phoning Tel: 35 133.

> *Directions:* From the 1A roadway (Aruba's large, two-lane north-south traffic artery), turn at the entrance to Oranjestad towards the two large supermarkets Pueblo and Ling & Sons (on the corner of the futuristic Ing Fatum Insurance building). Don't follow the street to the supermarkets but head straight on to the gravel road inland. After around 300 metres (325 yards) is the Aruba Sailcart building.

Scuba Diving

Many diving areas off Aruba's coast are among the best in the Caribbean. One of the main reasons for this is the clarity of the water; under water, visibility is up to 30 metres (100 feet). Water temperatures are also very pleasant.

A **coral reef** along the island's western coast runs from the north (California Reef) to Aruba's southern point (Baby Beach Reef) with diving depths from 5 to 45 metres.

The **Shipwreck** of the German freighter "Antilla" *(→ Sights) is also among the most popular scuba diving areas.*

In relation to this, there are a large number of diving schools and centres on Aruba. These offer excursions, but also courses to learn how to scubadive. The courses last three or four days, beginning with the first diving basics in the hotel swimming pools or theoretical training on the beach. Courses end with a test; if passed, scuba students receive a certificate with which they can rent out scuba equipment. Those who would like to take such a course should consider that it not only involves practical training but studying books as well. Books and training are in English without exception.

Prices: Group excursions start at $30 (£18) per tank filling. Training in the swimming pool costs $60 (£36). A basic course for scuba diving including examination/certification starts at $200 (£120).

A Selection of Diving Schools

> **Sea Scuba, Tel: 34 877; Pro Dive,** Tel: 27 778 or 29 059; **Peter's Divers Company,** Tel: 29 181; **Mermaid Sport Divers,** Tel: 35 546;

Red Sail Sports, Tel: 31 603; **Pelican Watersports,** Tel: 31 228 or 24 739.

Tennis

Every larger hotel has its own tennis court or courts available to guests. However, not all of the courts are in the best condition but they are all lighted, making it possible to play tennis after sunset when it's cooler. It is almost always possible to rent a racquet and tennis balls.

The eight tennis courts (two additional ones are planned) at the recently opened *Aruba Racquet Club* are in excellent condition. In this small, pleasant facility are also a restaurant, swimming pool, fitness room and a sports shop. The hard courts with a rubberised surface all have floodlights. Tourists can also play tennis here if courts are available. One hour costs $10 (£6) per court including lighting. The office is open from 7:30 am to noon and 2 to 11 pm. For reservations and information, phone Tel: 60 215.

> *Directions:* The Aruba Racquet Club is situated around 250 metres (275 yards) northeast of the last high rise hotel. The access road is across from the last high rise hotel. Turn left at the first dusty roadway. The facility can be recognised from the beach road by its floodlight poles and the strange octagonal form of the clubhouse roof.

Waterskiing

With the selection of waterskiing options Aruba's large organisers are the market leaders; they have most small boat owners under contract as subcontractors.

Pelican Watersports: at the high rise hotels, Tel: 31 228 or 24 739, or *Red Sail Sports* near the low rise hotels, Tel: 31 603, offer waterskiing at the nearby beaches. One half hour costs $50 (£30); one full hour, $80 (£48).

Windsurfing

With *Fisherman's Hut (→ Sights),* Aruba has one of the best calm-water areas for windsurfers in the world. The wind statistics on Aruba, "the island under the wind" is phenomenal. There are hardly any days where the wind is calm and on four of every five days, the wind reaches an average speed exceeding 15 knots. The already strong wind heats up over the island and with this, increases in speed. then, at its highest speed, it sweeps over the undeveloped, flat area near Fisherman's Hut and out over the sea. Other advantages for windsurfers: the warm, clean water and the fact that the water is only hip-deep for 400 metres along the beach be 300 metres out to sea. Beginners and experts alike have optimal training conditions here. If taking a fall into the water, it is easy to bet back onto the board and continue. At Fisherman's Hut, four **Surf Stations** have established themselves.

First, the *Vela Surfstation* is located at the southern end of Fisherman's Hut. The Vela station rents out Mistral surfboards with Neil-Pryde sails. However, one problem is that the station is directly in front of the hotels and a marina for ships has also been built in the harbour. The chaotic winds caused by the hotels makes it more complicated to sail out from the station and back.

Happy Windsurfing also has a station at Fisherman's Hut, renting out F2 surfboards with North sails. The staff at Happy build their station every morning at 10, having transported it with two trailers, and dismantle it again at 5 every evening.

Sailboard Vacation is the name of the next surfstation, the largest station in the Caribbean, renting out 130 Bic surfboards and lots more UP sails.

Roger's Windsurf Palace is a small, good station. Roger is the only 'local' who operates a surf station. He competed in the 1992 Olympic Games in Barcelona for Aruba. In his friendly station, Roger rents out Fanatic equipment. He also rents out several apartments and a fantastic villa directly sea-side.

On Aruba, renting surfing equipment is rather expensive in comparison to other surfing destinations around the world. If the equipment is booked on Aruba, expect to pay around $250 (£150) for one week and $400 (£240) for two weeks, regardless of the station. It is somewhat less expensive if booked in advance from home. Of course, it is also possible to rent equipment by the hour at the hotels or the above stations. One hour costs $20 (£12); two hours $35 (£21).

Sunscreen

Every day, the sun shines almost eleven hours on Aruba — not only dangerous for visitors with fair skin. The constant winds detract from the sun's intensity this close to the equator, making it go unnoticed. When it is apparent, it's too late. Do not forget to pack an ample supply of sunscreen. Sunscreen factors 4, 6 and 12 are not sufficient for Aruba. Factor 30 is appropriate for sensitive areas like the nose and shoulders and factor 25 for the rest of the body. After preliminary tanning, the protection factor can be reduced to 15. Waterproof sunscreen is available in all hotels and souvenir shops and is most reasonably priced in the supermarkets (factor 15, waterproof, 200 ml for around 13 florin).

Supermarkets

To take some pressure off the travel budget, it can be a good idea to cook, at least occasionally. The selection at supermarkets, especially the two biggest "Ling & Sons" and "Pueblo" right next to each other, is huge and leaves nothing to be desired. Foods are mainly imported from the US, the Netherlands, Venezuela and Argentina, but also from Germany. Prices are generally higher.

■ **Ling & Sons,** Italiestraat 26, Tel: 32 370
■ **Pueblo,** L. G. Smith Blvd.

Open Monday to Saturday from 8 am to 8 pm; Sundays, 9 am to 1 pm. All in all, the two large supermarkets are pretty much alike.

> *Directions by Car:* At the northern entrance to Oranjestad on L. G. Smith Blvd. across from the drive to the low rise hotels, the last traffic light before or the first after Oranjestad, on the corner of the "Ing Fatum" heading inland.

> *Directions by Bus from Malmok or the Hotels:* The bus will stop on the corner of L. G. Smith Blvd. mentioned above on request, diagonally across from "Pueblo" and "Ling & Sons". When taking the bus back, be sure to note that the bus does not stop directly in front of the Pueblo supermarket even though tourists repeatedly attempt to flag the bus down here. Around 150 metres (175 yards) towards the city centre in front of the "Interbank Aruba" and across from the hotel school is the bus stop.

> For departure times: → *Buses*

Another supermarket which is easily accessible by bus is:

■ **Supermercado Kong Ling** on Havenstraat in Oranjestad, diagonally behind the Seaport Village Mall at the Sonesta Hotel.

■ However, the small **Schooner Market** along the harbour with its fruit and vegetable stands, a butcher and a fish stand is rather close by, right across from the bus stop in front of "Wendy's". When coming by bus, get off either in front of "Lover's Ice Cream" or wait for the last stop.

Kong Ling is open Monday, Friday and Saturday from 8 am to 6:30 pm; Tuesdays, Wednesdays and Thursdays from 8 am to 6 pm with a daily lunch break from noon to 2 pm. Closed Sundays.

■ The small **Palm Beach** supermarket for tourists staying in Noord, Malmok and the high rise hotels could be of interest since it is readily accessible on foot from Noord and the hotels or by bicycle from Malmok.

> *Directions from Malmok:* Turn left at the first traffic light near "Papa's & Beer" inland. *From the high rise hotels:* From the "Americana", head inland across the intersection around 150 metres (175 yards) beyond the Esso service station.

Taxis

On Aruba, taxi prices are set so there are no taximeters. Taxis in all colours and in good condition without exception wait in front of the larger hotels and can be flagged down everywhere in Oranjestad. Be sure to ask the price before starting the trip to avoid misunderstandings. Drivers are allowed to take up to four passengers. If there happens not to be a taxi right in front of the hotel, one can be ordered by phoning Tel: 22 116 or 21 604 in Oranjestad or 45 160 or 46 602 in San Nicolas at any time.

The most important taxi fares

Airport — Low Rise Hotels: $12 (£7.20)
Airport — High Rise Hotels: $14 (£8.40)
Airport — Malmok: $18 (£10.80)
Airport — Oranjestad: $8 (£4.80)
Low Rise Hotels — Oranjestad: $5 (£3)
High Rise Hotels — Oranjestad: $7 (£4.20)
Malmok: — Oranjestad: $9 (£5.40)
Surcharges include $ (60p) for trips on Sundays and $1 (60p) for luggage. If four passengers share a taxi, many drivers charge $1 (60p) more. Taxi drivers also offer island tours and serve as guides. The hourly rate is subject to negotiation.

Telephone

There are no problems with the telephone lines on Aruba or with international connections. International calls are no problem when placed at the large *hotels* but, in addition to the highest charges, there is also a service charge which makes this option very expensive. The rates do go down a bit after 10 pm but this can be an inconvenient time to call, especially if phoning Europe.
The international country code for Great Britain is 00 44 followed by the number omitting the initial '0'; for the US and Canada, it is 00 1. Those calling Aruba from England must dial 00 297 8 followed by the phone number and 011 297 8 from the US and Canada. There are a number of public telephones in Oranjestad from which calls can be placed using telephone cards. Telephone cards are available in the Setar Teleshops.
Setar Telecommunications offers telephone and fax communications which are much less expensive than using these services in hotels. The Setar shops are centrally located: the first is at the Hyatt Hotel parking area (→ *Accommodation).* The second is next to the main postal building in Oranjestad on J. E. Irausquinplein (→ *Postal System).* The third telephone shop is in Oranjestad

behind the Seaport Village Mall at the Sonesta Hotel on Schelpstraat, Strada 2. The shops are open Monday to Saturday from 8 am to 11 pm. In all the shops, a three-minute call to Europe costs around $15 (£9) regardless of the time of day. A five-minute call costs $22 (£13.20), the minimum being three minutes.

These shops also offer fax service, whereby one page costs $5 (£3).

Phoning the US from Aruba is much less expensive. A three-minute long distance call to New York costs $8 (£4.80) and as little as $6 (£3.60) after 7 pm. It is also possible to place calls from the *main post office (→ Postal System)*. However, there is only one telephone. The cabin is to the left of the main entrance. In some areas on Aruba, there are meanwhile telephones which accept credit cards. A PIN is required for this.

Time of Day

Aruba has *Atlantic Standard Time* throughout the year with no time difference from summer to winter. Therefore, Aruba is 4 hours behind Greenwich Mean Time in winter and 5 hours behind in summer. In Aruba (Bonaire and Curaçao) it is 6 or 7 am when it's noon in London. It is 1 hour ahead of Eastern Standard time in winter and the same as EST in summer.

Tipping

Officially, tips are a *service charge* on Aruba. Usually, these are just as officially listed on bills and thus, included in the total. If this is not the case, then a tip from 10 to 15% of the total amount is appropriate. A notice of whether or not service is included can most often be found at the lower right of restaurant menus.

Of course every waitperson, hotel staff member etc will be pleased with a gratuity for exceptional service. Again, 10 to 15% is appropriate. If no service charge is included on the bill, a tip should not be forgotten. Leaving no tip is considered extremely rude, unless the service was extremely bad. Keep in mind that, as in the US for example, waitpersons earn low wages since expected tips are calculated into their earnings. On Aruba, as in the states, hourly wages lie between $2 and $3 (£1.20 and £1.80).

Tourism Office

Aruba's government is increasingly attempting to market the island as independent. Thus, the **Aruba Tourism Authority** is represented more and more at tourism trade fairs and is making efforts to help tour organisers and individual tourists alike in planning holidays.

In both tourism offices on Aruba, the staff is very helpful. Informational materials in English about the island can be found here. If contacted by fax, an answer can take several days (sometimes, a second or third fax is necessary). In addition, the office has a list of private accommodation including the prices charged *(→ Accommodation).*

Tourism Offices on Aruba

The **Aruban Tourism Authority** maintains two offices on the island: one is next to the Sonesta Hotel on Oranjestad's yacht harbour (Tel: +2978 23 788. The other is a larger office at the northern entrance to Oranjestad: Aruba Tourism Authority, L. G. Smith Blvd. 172, Oranjestad, Aruba; Tel: +2978 23 777, Fax: +2978 34 702.
Directions: Turn right at the traffic light in front of the "Ing Fatum" insurance building (the same direction as the two large supermarkets). Keep left beyond the insurance building. The office is housed in a beautiful villa with nice balconies (the building is illuminated during the evening).

Tourism Offices Abroad

Canada: 1801 Eglington Avenue West, Suite 109, Toronto, Ontario M6E 2H7; Tel: (416) 782-9954, Fax: (416) 782-6021.
USA: 521 5th Ave, 12th floor, New York, NY 10175, Tel: (212) 246-3030 or toll-free in the US 1-800-TO-ARUBA, Fax: (212) 557-1614.

Tourist Information

In the Seaport Village Mall (next to the Sonesta Hotel) is a stand in the central corridor, offering a lot of information on activities on the island. Piles of flyers are available at this stand and in the hotels as well. These flyers advertise the seemingly endless opportunities: catamaraning, island tours by bus, a show here, a party there, an all-star performance, an Aruban beauty contest and much, much more. The events and activities can also be booked at the Seaport Village Mall as well as in the *Tourist Office.*
In addition to these, there are also several attractive brochures like *Aruba Nights, Aruba events* or simply *aruba,* which contain both useful and less useful information. These brochures can be found in almost every shop (or at least those which advertise in these brochures). free of charge.
The billboard, a free flyer, offers current information every day. It is financed through advertising and announces special events. It is definitely worthwhile to take a glance at The billboard. This has the most current information and

is, therefore, often out of stock. The best time and place to find one is in Oranjestad early in the morning. → *Tourism Office*

Travel Documents

Aruba is a very friendly island towards foreigners and is dependent on tourism as the island's main source of income *(→ Tourism; Economy).* For this reason, there are not all too many formalities for visitors to enter Aruba. Tourists from Europe need only a passport valid past the planned date of departure and a return ticket for stays lasting up to three months. For renting a car or motorcycle *(→ Car Rental; Motorcycles),* visitors will need a valid driving licence.

Those intending to bring along a pet must have a certificate of good health from a recognised veterinarian to present upon arrival.

Those who wish to work on the island should enter as a normal tourist and take care of the necessary formalities for a longer stay and a work permit once on the island. It is not all that difficult to be granted a work permit as a foreigner. Those interested should either bring along ample capital and, by starting a new enterprise, create jobs or they should work in a profession which is in short supply on Aruba. Detailed information is available from the *Department of Economic Affairs, Commerce and Industry,* L. G. Smith Blvd. 15, Oranjestad, Aruba, Tel: 21 181, Fax: 34 494.

Travelling to Aruba

Aruba has been a popular destination for North and South American tourists for around twenty years, but Europeans are gradually discovering Aruba as well. As a result, charter flights are beginning to be offered.

Up to the summer of 1993, flights to Aruba were the domain of the Dutch airline **KLM** due to the traditionally close ties between the Netherlands and their former colonies in the Caribbean. Even today, numerous flights depart from Amsterdam; and this, almost daily during the winter months. A direct flight from Amsterdam lasts around ten hours; around twelve hours with a stop-over on St. Maarten. A return (round-trip) ticket officially costs about $1,520 (£912). In travel agencies offering discount flights, such a ticket can cost up to 35% less.

The *Reina Beatrix Airport* offers good connections with the US and South America. The prices quoted below change constantly but do serve as an indication of airline ticket prices. All airlines are represented at the airport and price information is available by contacting the airline offices.

KLM offers up to nine flights a week during the winter schedule from October to the end of March. These are either direct flights or with a stop-over on Sint

Maarten. **Amreican Airlines** offers almost daily flights go Aruba from US airports via Miami or Houston. The **Aeropostal** Airline flies daily, sometimes several times daily, to and from Caracas Venezuela. A ticket costs around $120 (£72). Twice a week, Aeropostal flights depart Aruba for Santo Domingo, Venezuela, costing $250 (£150). In addition, Aeropostal offers two connections to the US: four times a week to Atlanta (costing around $350/£210) and three times a week to Orlando, Florida.

Aruba's national airline, **Air Aruba,** is shaken by crises. The ambitious project by island politicians to establish the island's own airline cost the Aruban taxpayers a great deal of money. At times, Air Aruba offers flights to and from Europe. At present, the airline is concentrating on flights to and from the US and South America. Thus, there are daily flights connecting Aruba with New York (for $380/£228). Twice a week, the airline flies to Baltimore and once a week to Miami (for $340/£204). Connections to South America are also good: seven flights a week for $112 (£67) to Caracas, twice a week to Bogatá and three times a week to Medellin, Columbia. In addition to these, there are two flights to São Paulo, Brazil for around $800 (£480).

Viasa lands at the Reine Beatrix Airport six times a week: three times from Houston for $500 (£300) and three times from Caracas for $112 (£67).

Avianca flies less frequently: three times a week to Bogatá for around $250 (£150) and once to Barquilla for $220 (£132).

Vaccinations

Tropical diseases are unknown on Aruba. For this reason, no vaccinations are necessary; not even for yellow fever or malaria. An exception: entering Aruba from an infected area. Another risk: AIDS has not stopped from infecting the island paradise of Aruba. Official figures on HIV-positive Arubans are not available, but several times a year, the government initiates a campaign to educate the populace.

Vegetation

Five hundred millimetres (19½ inches) of precipitation each year does not allow for lush, tropical vegetation. For this reason, a large portion of Aruba has the character of a western North American landscape, like that in Arizona. Where enough soil is present, it is predominantly *shrubs* and *cactuses* that grow. There are around 500 types of plants on Aruba, but what is most characteristic of the landscapes are the cactuses. In the island's interior, the cactuses virtually form forests, albeit not very dense. There are cactuses on the island that have reached a height of 13 metres (43 feet). Local residents plant these close together to form a natural fence.

the island that have reached a height of 13 metres (43 feet). Local residents plant these close together to form a natural fence.

The island's symbol is the low *watapana tree,* the *divi divi,* the crown of which grows in the direction of the wind. Therefore, it always points west. Earlier, the wild divi divi also had economic significance: its yellow fruit contains a high level of tannin which was used in tanning hides. Today, synthetic chemicals have replaced this.

Aloe — for health and beauty

Aloe, originally from the arid regions of Africa, grows on Aruba. In 1860, aloe was first cultivated on Aruba to process its juice into oil, cosmetics and medications. For a time, Aruba produced 70% of the world's aloe as recently as the first half of this century. Today, its economical significance has dropped dramatically. Still, Aloe can be found everywhere on the island.

Also characteristic of the island's flora are the *flamboyant trees* and *palm trees* — the *coconut palm* and the *royal palm.* In addition, *hibiscus, lemon, papaya* and *mango trees* can be found in many gardens. All the trees, palms and flowering plants can only survive if irrigated. The large salt extraction plant yields enough fresh water.

Weights and Measures

The weights and measures on Aruba vary between several international weights and measures even though the official system is the metric system. However, the high number of North Americans on Aruba and the numerous US products in the supermarkets and stores are in pounds, ounces etc. Here, a brief conversion chart:

Weights:	**Volume**	**Distance**
1 ounce = 28.35 g	1 quart = 0.946 litre	1 yard = 91.44 cm
1 pound = 453 g	1 gallon = 3.785 litre	1 mile = 1.60934 km

Aruba's Cities and Towns — An Overview

■ Oranjestadt

with a population of around 25,000, Oranjestad is Aruba's capital. The airport, the yacht harbour and port all lie near Oranjestad. There is one shopping mall after the next in Oranjestad not only with jewellers, boutiques, perfume shops and shoe stores but restaurants, a few pubs and the city's few museums. The largest supermarkets, the main post office and countless Aruban businesses offices can be found in Oranjestad and of course, all governmental offices. Oranjestad is also Aruba's touristic hub where tourists stroll the streets, buy souvenirs, rent boats or eat ice cream or a quick meal.

Towards the sea, Oranjestad is characterised by Dutch façades. The shopping malls are all pleasant in Caribbean colours with imitation Dutch architecture. However, farther east, things look quite different. There, the houses of local residents can be found and some areas are not at all quaint.

The island's oldest building, *Fort Zoutman,* stands in Oranjestad with its cannons which once protected the island's population. On Wilhelminastraat

The ABC islands offer endless opportunities to challenge the wind and waves

are several more beautiful houses which tell tales of the past. These, however, are gradually decaying.

Important Telephone Numbers

Police Station Oranjestad, Wilhelminastraat 40, Tel: 24 000
Fire Department, Sabana Berde 71, Tel: 21 108
Post Office, Irausquinplein 9, Tel: 21 900
District Physicians, D. S, Bermudez (general practitioner), Tel: 38 211; B. A. R. Heinze (general practitioner), Tel: 32 364

■ San Nicolas

San Nicolas is, so to speak, the opposite of Oranjestad. There are only a few shops, relatively few offices and no Dutch façades at all. San Nicolas is a working class city. Up to the time when the Lago Oil Company decided to build a refinery due to the natural harbour, this town was more or less a collection of huts. This changed seemingly overnight when one wooden house was built after the other in 1925; the city grew rapidly. Only the fewest residents came from Aruba; most were from other Caribbean islands. Over the years, the houses were torn down and replaced by stone houses. However, some of the old, colourful houses can still be seen in some parts of San Nicolas.

When the refinery was shut down in 1985, San Nicolas all but became a ghost town. The rate of unemployment skyrocketed to around 20% and many of San Nicolas' residents left the island. Since the refinery was reopened, the city's future has become brighter. In addition, many of the city's residents work in hotels, restaurants and casinos or on the beaches along the western coast. One special aspect of San Nicolas is the district of Seroe Colorado (→ *Sights*) on the island's southern point, south of the refinery, built by the oil refinery for its managers and skilled labour.

Important Telephone Numbers

Police Station San Nicolas, Bernhardstraat, Tel: 45 000
Fire Department, Marktstraat, Tel: 46 538
Postal Station San Nicolas, Tel: 45 009
District Physicians: E. J. M Boderie, Tel: 45 155; M. Cheung, E. Westrate, C E. Zaandam (all 3, general practitioners), Tel: 48 833

■ Noord

The small town of Noord owes its existence to a deadly plague. This first flared up in the population which lived near Alto Vista (→ *Sights*). For fear of contracting the disease, the people no longer visited the church in Alto Vista, many moved away and built a new church in Noord: St. Annakerk (→ *Sights*) with its neo-Gothic carved altar. There is an interesting cemetery adjacent to the church. Noord increasingly developed into a new tourism hub on Aruba and with new shops and businesses, restaurants and several new hotels, the town gradually grew closer and closer to the chain of hotels along the western coast. Steps are also being taken to improve the town's infrastructure. Thus, sidewalks were added last year in the *Palm Beach* district and street lamps were installed. This in turn made for an increased number of tourists who stroll the streets in Noord and shop in its stores, which, in turn, caused a small shopping centre to be built. However, other than the St. Annakerk, and other than the local flair, restaurants and shops, Noord does not have any noteworthy sights.

Important Telephone Numbers

> *Police Station Noord,* Tel: 78 000
> *Fire Department (for Oranjestad),* Tel: 21 108
> *Postal Station Noord,* Tel: 60 280
> *District Physician:* T. H. K. Lin (general practitioner), Tel: 61 522

■ Santa Cruz

The first to settle in Santa Cruz were the Spanish conquistadors. It was here that the first Catholic cross was erected (thus the name Santa Cruz) and this, on the site that was considered the central point of the island. The cross which can be seen here today dates back only to 1968.

Santa Cruz, with a population of around 10,000 today, does indeed lie approximately at the island's centre.

Important Telephone Numbers

> *Fire Department* (for Oranjestad), Tel: 21 108
> *District Physicians:* E. De Cuba (general practitioner), Tel: 25 666; A. S. Ridderstap (general practitioner), Tel: 28 017

■ Savaneta

Savaneta's golden age lies well over 100 years in the past. But then as now, the military characterised the town's profile. Due to its ideal coastline, the Spanish laid anchor here while conquering the island. Later, it would be the Dutch. The commanders became the governors of the island here, thus the name *"Commandeursbaai"*. Later, the governor moved to the official seat in Oranjestad. Today, the Dutch marines have a base in Savaneta.

Important Telephone Numbers

> *Police Station Savaneta,* Tel: 47 000
> *District Physician:* J. J. Geerman-Tromp (general practitioner), Tel: 47 224

Bonaire

General Information

"Bonaire is for lovers" is the title of one brochure. And moreover: *"Bonaire is for lovers. Lovers of sunshine, of sand and the sea. For lovers and lovers of solitude."* There's little more to add.

Eighty kilometres (50 miles) off the South American coast lies the island of Bonaire, the easternmost island under the wind. Bonaire is situated 100 kilometres (63 miles) east of Curaçao, 140 kilometres (88 miles) east of Aruba and belongs to the Netherlands politically; the head of state is the Dutch Queen. Bonaire has the physical shape of a boomerang and is 38 kilometres (24 miles) in length, between 6.5 and 11.5 kilometres (4 and 7 miles) wide and has an area of 288 square kilometres (112 square kilometres), making it the second largest of the Dutch Antilles. Its geographical location is 12°5' north latitude and 86°25' west longitude. The southern portion of the island is flat and arid while the northern regions are more hilly. **Brandaris Hill** is the island's highest elevation, reaching 235 metres (770 feet). The island's northern regions are used in agriculture while the southern portions are reserved for salt extraction. Bonaire's capital city is **Kralendijk,** a small city with a population of 2,500.

Accommodation

In respect to its hotels, Bonaire is a paradise. There are no huge cement hotel blocks as is the case on Aruba. Since tourism has developed only gradually and remains on a comparatively low level, there is no need for high rise hotels along the beaches. In addition, preserving the intact environment is emphasised on Bonaire and harmony with the landscape plays an important role in planning any new buildings. This all has its price. Hotel rooms start at around $100 (£64) per night for a double. During high season — from December 16 to mid April — prices double in many of the hotels. The following is a list of hotels equipped with a fax machine:

Hotels on Bonaire

Sorobon Beach Resort, Sorobon, Fax: +599 7 5363. The Sorobon Beach Resort is Bonaire's only nudist club complex. The 30 wooden bungalows lie secluded on Lac Bay.

Sand Dollar Beach Club, Kaya Gob. N. Debrot, Fax: +599 7 876. An elegant hotel with a swimming pool and tennis courts, this hotel's

BONAIRE

Caribbean Sea

Boca Kokolishi

Boca Bartol

Slagbaai

Flamingo
Reserve

Playa Frans

National Park

Lake
Goto

Rincon

Playa Chikitu

Playa Grandi

Boca Onima

Boca Oliva

Punta Blancu

Klein Bonaire

Kralendijk

Sea Park

Bachelor's Beach

Lac Bay
Sorobo

Pink Beach

*Sorobon
Beach*

Flamingo
Reserve

Obelisk
Slave Huts

Willemstoren

restaurant *Green Parrot* is very popular. A diving station is adjacent. 75 Apartments.

Harbour Village Beach Resort, Kaya Gob. N. Debrot, Fax: +599 7 7507. The only luxury hotel on Bonaire's nicest beach. A canal leads to the hotel's own yacht harbour. Restaurant, diving station. 72 rooms.

Captain Don's Habitat, Kaya Gob. N. Debrot, Fax: +599 7 8240. With around 60 rooms, this hotel is relatively new. It is popular with scuba divers.

Sunset Beach Resort, Kaya Gob. N. Debrot, Fax: +599 7 8118 or information and reservations in the Netherlands: Tel/Fax: +31 5720 61085. The old restaurant under a palm roof is very popular. This old hotel with around 150 rooms has a charm all its own. Many of the guests are 'regulars' here.

Buddy Beach & Dive Resort, Kaya Gob. N. Debrot, Fax: +599 7 8647 or information and reservations in the Netherlands: +31 5413 55474, Fax: +31 5413 55236. A rather new complex with 20 apartments, popular with scuba divers.

Coral Regency Resort, Kaya Gob. N. Debrot, Fax: +599 7 5680. The beautiful view of the sea never ceases to be fascinating. The 33 rooms scattered among two-storey villas all have their own kitchen. A generous, exclusive complex.

Lac Bay Resort, Sorobon, Fax: +599 7 5198 or information and reservations in the Netherlands: +31 1653 83970, Fax: +31 1653 88027. Ten rooms are housed in three wooden buildings. It is foremost visitors in search of peace and solitude who prefer this hotel in a secluded location on Lac Bay.

Carib Inn, J. A. Abraham Boulevard, Fax: +599 7 5295. It takes a great deal of luck to get a room in this hotel since it is usually booked solid months in advance. Divers especial like this hotel.

Divi Flamingo Beach, J. A. Abraham Boulevard, Fax: +599 7 8238. Information and reservations in Great Britain, Tel: +44 453 835805, Fax: +44 453 835525. An old, charming hotel with tropical gardens. 105 rooms.

Bonaire Caribbean Club, Tourist Road, Fax: +599 7 7900. Information and reservations in the Netherlands: Tel: +31 3461 2092, Fax: +31 3461 3126

In addition, the Bonaire Tourist Office in the Netherlands has a current list of all those who rent out apartments and bungalows. Lydia Havemann will be happy to help further (→ *Tourist Office*).

Climate

Without exaggeration: Bonaire has summer 365 days a year; there is hardly a day with clouds or rain. The average temperature lies around 27.5°C (81.5°F) throughout the year with 500 mm (19½ inches) of precipitation annually. The climate is considered good for the circulation.

Customs Regulations

Each person over 21 is allowed to bring 200 cigarettes and a bottle of alcoholic beverages into Bonaire duty-free in addition to personal items.

Drinking Water

The drinking water on Bonaire is processed by a salt extraction plant. It can be drunk without reservation. In contrast, don't drink the water that comes from any wells. This water is for irrigation or the wells are merely for decoration.

Driving and Car Rental

Bonaire is a paradise for drivers; not to say the roads are especially good and virtually free of traffic, no. There are no traffic lights on Bonaire. The traffic signs are European standard and driving is on the right-hand side of the road. In addition, there are no strict driving conventions on Bonaire.

Numerous companies rent out cars. For this, renters must present a valid, national driving licence and pay a deposit. Renting a compact car on Bonaire will cost around $30 (£18) per day; for a jeep, expect to pay around $50 (£30) per day. Visitors should most definitely take advantage of the opportunity to rent a car on Bonaire since bus service is not exactly the best on this island and a taxi will prove expensive after a while, especially when visitors plan on travelling around the island.

Car Rental Agencies

AB Car Rental, Flamingo Airport, Tel: 8980; **Avis Car Rental,** J. A. Abraham Boulevard 4, Tel: 8033; **Budget Car Rental,** Kaya Grandi 96, Tel: 8487; **Camel Car Rental,** Kaya Betico Croes 28, Tel: 5120; **Dollar Car Rental,** Kaya Grandi 86, Tel: 8888; **Everts Car Rental,** Sabana, Tel: 8099; **Good Wheels Car Rental,** Kaya Pabou 6, Tel: 8724; **Sun and Sand Car Rental,** Kaya Industria 17, Tel: 8677; **Sunray Car Rental,** Flamingo Airport, Tel: 5600; **Trupial Car Rental.** Kaya Grandi 96, Tel: 8487

Electricity → *Aruba / Electricity*

Entering Bonaire

Those who do not plan on staying more than three months on Bonaire need only official identification or a passport. For US citizens, a birth certificate, alien registration card or naturalisation papers is sufficient. Canadian visitors must have a passport or birth certificate.

All visitors must confirm they have reserved accommodation and present an onward or return ticket. Guests to the island who would like to stay longer than three months must apply for a visa at the Immigration Office. It is better to first enter as a 'normal' tourist (if not bringing along an entire household's worth of luggage) and apply for a visa after arrival.

History

Amerigo Vespucci officially discovered Bonaire in the year 1499 — the island had, however, already been inhabited by Arawak Indians for centuries. Vespucci named the island after an Arawak work "bonnah" which means as much as "flat land".

The Spanish attempted to colonise the island between 1527 and 1634, but this attempt was not terribly successful. Then, the Dutch took over Bonaire in 1634 and established a military base on the island. The Dutch West Indian Company spurred on salt production on the island after the Spanish denied the Dutch the salt they needed so desperately for pickling fish. In order to establish some agriculture in addition to this, the Dutch brought around 100 African slaves to the island. The company remained active on the island for 160 years.

During the early 19th century, the British occupied Bonaire, yet without paying much attention to their new possession. The consequence was that Bonaire often suffered under French and English pirate attacks. In 1816, the Dutch gained control over the island once more and would not relinquish this power again. During the subsequent period, however, they had a lot to do in solving problems on the island. For instance, when slavery was abolished in 1863, many companies became unprofitable. Numerous residents left the island in the 90 years to follow and emigrated to Curaçao or Aruba to work for the oil refinery.

During the 1950s, economic and social life on Bonaire took an upswing as tourism came to Bonaire. The numbers were (and comparatively, still are) humble; yet Bonaire could claim an economic boost. The Bonaire Petroleum Corporation built a terminal in which oil from large tankers was distributed among smaller vessels.

Even early on, it was recognised on Bonaire that an intact environment is an important argument for tourism. Thus, as early as 1979, the surrounding waters were declared a nature reserve. Later, establishing parks and nature reserves on the island itself would follow.

Language → *Aruba / Language*

Medical Care

There is a small **hospital** on Bonaire (Tel: 14), located on Kaya Soeur Bartola in Kralendijk only a short walk north from the 'city centre'. The hospital is equipped with a decompression chamber for scuba diving accidents.

Money

The same currency is used on Bonaire as on Curaçao, the Netherlands Antilles guilder (NAG or NAfl). The exchange rate to the US dollar is set, as on Aruba. One US dollar = 1.77 NAfl. It is possible to pay in US dollars

Slave huts on Bonaire — remnants of Bonaire's colonial past

everywhere; some banks accept Eurocheques. Banks are usually open Monday to Friday from 8:30 am to noon and 2 to 4 pm.

Most shops and all hotels and car rental agencies accept credit cards like Mastercard (Eurocard), Visa and American Express. However, some businesses charge up to a 9% surcharge when payment is made by credit card. When renting a car, it is a good idea to pay by credit card since the deposit is then taken care of.

Nature

Bonaire stands out for its pristine nature — especially below the water's surface. The diving areas surrounding the island are among the most beautiful in the world and definitely the most beautiful in the Caribbean. It was recognised early on, just how valuable this untouched nature is for the island's economy. Thus, the *Bonaire Marine Park* was established in 1979, for example. The intent of this was to prevent damage to the fragile coral and fish through numerous divers.

On the island itself, visitors are confronted with a sooner bizarre side of nature: beaches, mangrove forests, rugged coastal cliffs with bizarre bays, a lowland plateau to the north. Just about every type of landscape can be found on Bonaire, which visitors would expect from the Caribbean.

The *Washington Slagbaai National Park* is situated in the island's northern regions and is the habitat of over 190 species of birds like the *yellow-winged Amazon parrot,* the *trupial,* the *pink flamingo,* or the green *pygmy parrot.* This beautiful bird sanctuary is also a reason that an increasing number of birdwatchers and ornithologists visit Bonaire. The pink flamingos that still find a few places where they can nest undisturbed are also a treat to the eye. After the southern point of the island was declared a *bird sanctuary,* the flamingo population, which had drastically fallen off world-wide, recovered to the point that there are now around 13,000 flamingos on Bonaire — with this, there are more flamingos than people.

However, the *lizards* are the most abundant animals on the island.

The *flora* on Bonaire is influenced by the low levels of precipitation and therefore, predominantly comprises cactuses like the *barrel cactus,* the *torch cactus* or the bizarre *saguaro,* which can grow up to 10 metres (34 feet) high. In addition, as on Aruba, the famous *divi divi* trees grow on Bonaire. Their branches grow westwards.

The People of Bonaire

Almost 12,000 people live on Bonaire. Their complexions are generally darker than that of the Aruban population *(→ Aruba / People).* This is evidence of the

African slaves who — in contrast to Aruba — were brought to Bonaire and later mixed with the population *(→ History).*

Postal System

The post office is located on the corner of Reina Wilhelmina Square in Kralendijk, diagonally across from the ABN Bank. Official address: J. A. Abraham Blvd., Kralendijk. The post office is open from 7:30 am to noon and 1:30 to 5 pm. Money transfers can be made only from 1:30 to 4 pm.

Scuba Diving

There might be tourists who consider Bonaire a sleepy, relatively boring island. There might be tourists who don't think the beaches are nice enough. It is difficult to complain about the weather, but the most convincing argument for Bonaire is the beauty of the underwater world surrounding it. Bonaire's diving areas count among the three most beautiful regions in the world. Even those who don't scubadive can don a face mask and go snorkelling. The crystal clear water surrounding the island with visibility up to 30 metres (100 feet) is home to several thousand types of fish living in the coral reef's crevices.

The island government quickly recognised that protecting nature, especially the underwater world, is absolutely necessary. Spear-fishing or removing any fish or coral (without a special licence) was prohibited by law as early as 1971. **Bonaire Marine Park** was established in 1979 to protect the sensitive coral and marine life. Diving stations have been set up surrounding Bojen Island to ease tying up diving boats since anchoring along Bonaire's coasts is prohibited. In light of the 600 dives per day, this measure is also urgently needed if the beautiful underwater world is to be preserved. Even touching coral under water or feeding the fish is prohibited; diving guides pay special attention to enforce this. Fishermen must be licenced and must provide proof of where they caught their catch.

One book is especially good for scuba divers: the "Guide to the Bonaire Marine Park" by Tom van't Hof (in English).

A sandbar stretches along the island's eastern coast and around 12 metres (40 feet) from the beach is a 'step' down to a coral reef at a depth of around 30 metres (100 feet) then another 'step' down to the ocean floor. The seas are sooner rough on the east side of the island and only in October and November is the water more calm.

On the island's western side, are countless diving sites at varying depths. Divers can also explore the reefs and shipwrecks here. Around 1.5 kilometres (1 mile) from Kralendijk lies the island of **Klein Bonaire,** where divers can also find good diving areas.

Snorkelling: Those who would like to snorkel can find especially nice areas at *Nukove, Boca Slagbaai, Playa Funchi, Windsock Steep* and around *Klein Bonaire*. One special aspect is that Bonaire has excellent diving areas directly accessible from its beaches.

In total, fourteen diving stations can be found on Bonaire. They offer everything imaginable related to scuba diving. The competition is stiff making it worthwhile sometimes to bargain with prices. The prices for scuba diving (tank fillings) vary from $25 to $50 (£15 to £30) if providing one's own equipment.

The following are the addresses of the diving stations which can also be helpful in organising an entire trip to Bonaire since most are associated with a hotel or at least work in close co-operation with hotel owners.

Diving Stations on Bonaire

Bonaire Scuba Centre, PO Box 200, Tel: +599 7 8846. This diving centre lies near the Black Durgon Inn Resort and offers: courses, diving certification, advanced and specialist courses. In addition, they offer packages for beginners, advanced divers and snorkellers. It is specialised in excursions on the eastern coast and to the shipwrecks.

Buddy Dive Resort, Kaya Gob. Debrot 85, Tel: +599 7 5080, Fax: -7080. Buddy offers everything that a scuba diver could desire. All types of courses, excursions and certification and has specialised on underwater photography. The station rents out diving equipment and handles repairs.

Carib Inn Dive Shop, PO Box 68, Tel: +599 7 8819, Fax: -5295. Bruce Bowker's diving station is completely equipped and offers all types of diving opportunities. The station is near Carib Inn. Bruce also sells diving equipment.

Dee Scarr's, "Touch the Sea", Tel: +599 7 8529. Dee Scarr has specialised in small groups and even individuals. He also offers the special PADI "Touch the Sea" certification.

Dive Inn, Kaya C.E.B. Hellmund 27, Tel: +599 7 8761, Fax: -8513. The Dive Inn station lies off Kralendijk Bay, foremost serving guests staying at the Sunset Inn and the Sunset Oceanfront Apartments. The selection includes all types of excursions and courses. Scuba fans can also buy or rent diving equipment, or have equipment repaired. In addition, Dive Inn also offers sailing and snorkelling equipment. Even fishing trips and water-skiing are available here along with **motorcycle rental.**

Great Adventures Bonaire, PO Box 312, Kralendijk, Tel: +599 7 7500, Fax: -7507. The Great Adventures station is at the Harbour Village Resort. A broad spectrum of courses are offered whether from a boat or from the beach. Rental equipment is available and this station also does repairs. Even night diving is offered.

Habitat Dive Centre, PO Box 88, Tel: +599 7 8290, Fax: -8240. This station lies near Captain Don's Habitat, offering a PADI 5-star programme. "Diving Freedom" is the special offer where it is possible to scuba dive 24 hours a day. It is also specialised in underwater photography in co-operation with Photo Tours.

Night Dive N.V., PO Box 333, Tel: +599 7 8330, Fax: -5230. The Night Dive station is near the Sunset Beach Hotel. All types of courses and excursions to various reefs and shipwrecks as well as picnic excursions are offered. Diving equipment can be purchased, rented or repaired here. Snorkelling is also possible.

Photo Tours N.V., Kaya Grandi 68, Tel: +599 7 8060, Fax: -8060. Photo Tours lies near the main shopping street in Kralendijk and is *the* specialist on the island when it comes to diving and photography or videography courses, offered either on an individual or group basis. Film can be developed on the same day. Cameras are available to either rent or buy. The selection of diving equipment is limited.

Patrick's Divers, Tel: +599 7 4080, Fax: -4080. The small station near Joe's Mini-Market offers all types of courses, however only originating from the beach. Diving equipment can be rented, purchased or repaired here.

Blue Divers, Tel: +599 7 6560. Blue divers is located nest to the Leeward Inn. The small station also offers all types of courses originating from the beach. Rental equipment is available.

Neal Watson's Bonaire Undersea Adventures, Kaya Gobernador N. Debrot 90, Tel: +599 7 5425, Fax: -5680. Neal Watson's station lies near the Coral Regency Resort. Among the large selection, the exquisite specialised excursions are exceptional. The diving tours originate from a boat or from the beach. Night diving is also offered.

Peter Hughes Dive Bonaire, Kralendijk, Tel: +599 7 8285, Fax: -8238. The diving station located at Divi Flamingo Beach Resort offers everything that a diver could want — all types of diving courses, even for advanced divers, photo tours and special photography and video courses.

Sand Dollar Dive and Photo, PO Box 175, Tel: +599 7 5252, Fax: -8760. As the name already says, this station is near the Sand Dollar Beach Club. All types of courses and excursions are offered here. What is exceptional are the advanced diving courses and life-saving courses. Along with photo tours, specialised photography and video courses are organised.

Shopping

Bonaire is not exactly a shopper's paradise. This is due to the island's size and is reflected in the selection in stores. What is refreshing on Bonaire, in contrast to its sister island of Aruba, is that shoppers will find more 'normal' articles on Bonaire and there isn't a string of luxury shops.

Business Hours: Monday to Saturday from 8 am to noon and 2 to 6 pm. Fridays, stores are open longer until 9 pm; this was established to accommodate beach-goers. When cruise ships dock in the harbour on Sundays, proprietors open their shops for an hour.

Bonaire's Sights — An Overview

Those who take enough time to discover Bonaire more intensively should rent a car. By car, the island can be explored in one day, allowing enough time to linger at especially attractive places. It is important to bring along ample drinking water and sunscreen.

■ Northern Route

The roadway from Kralendijk heading north, the *scenic road,* first leads past the hotels and the salt extraction plant. There are some excellent snorkelling or diving areas along this rugged section of coastline. Pay attention to the lizards while driving since they like to sun themselves on the roadway. Near the National Park Foundation Building is the opportunity to turn right and head inland towards *Rincon.* The crest of a hill offers a beautiful view of the eastern coast. Those who continue straight on at this fork will first pass the *Bonaire Petroleum Company* with the road to **Goto Lake,** Bonaire's inland saltwater lake. This is the best place to observe Bonaire's *flamingo* population. On the other roadway, drivers will reach *Rincon,* the island's oldest town where the slave families once lived. Beyond Rincon, a roadway forks off to the **Boca Onima Caves.** Six Arawak cave drawings can be seen there. In addition, there is a road from Rincon to **Washington Slagbaai National Park,** extending over the island's entire northern point. Returning from the park to Kralendijk leads through inland regions through the towns of **Noord Salija** and Antriol.

■ Southern Route

Bonaire's southern route first runs past the hotels, then the airport. The 213 metre (697 foot), three million watt *Trans World Radio* tower is very impressive. Its shortwave broadcasts reach almost every corner of the world.

Bonaire's southwestern coast is as good as paved over with hotels, villas and apartment complexes. Salt extraction plants dominate the coastal area's profile as seen from the coastal road. The salt flats shimmer pink and lavender in the sunshine, by all means an impressive sight. Farther south, the radiant white salt flats extend to the 'mountains'. There, visitors will also see three **obelisks** in blue, orange and white. Built in 1838, these serve seafarers in orientation. The small **slave huts** nearby are remnants from the times when salt was extracted by hand.

The **Flamingo Reserve** extends in Bonaire's southern regions. This is the habitat of the slender, pink birds which are quite at home next to the salt extraction plants.

Protection from the intense sunlight is a must on the ABC islands

On the island's southern tip, **Willemstoren,** Bonaire's lighthouse towers into the sky. And **Lac Bay** follows beyond the Sorobon complex and the mangrove swamps. Its clear water is inviting for underwater exploration. And that which looks like snowy mountains in the sunlight is actually a huge pile of shells near **Boca Cai.** The road back to Kralendijk leads through the town of **Nikiboko.**

Washington Slagbaai National Park

Over 190 species of birds live in Washington Slagbaai National Park, sharing the park with wild goats, donkeys and countless lizards. The park is open daily from 8 am to 5 pm, but no one is admitted after 3:30 pm. Admission costs $2 (£1.20); free of charge for children under 15. Across from the office is a small *museum* with finds from archaeological digs, geological explanations, pictures of birds and a collection of shells. A toilet can be found at the park entrance. However, there is nowhere to get food or water — be sure to bring along enough supplies.

Fishing, hunting, motorcycling, cycling and camping are all prohibited within the national park. The vegetation offers little diversity, the landscape is arid, dusty and only rocks and cactuses provide for contrast.

Walking Tours: There are two different sightseeing routes in the park: The route marked with yellow arrows is 34 kilometres (21 miles) long and the route marked with green arrows is 24 kilometres (15 miles) long. The yellow route can seem especially long in the tropical heat — be sure to bring along ample drinking water. The longer route also leads by Goto Lake, but the view from outside the park is better.

Sports and Recreation

Just about every type of sport or recreational activity in or on the water is possible on Bonaire. Of course, the highest on the hit list is scuba diving. Around eighty top-rate diving areas lie scattered around the small island *(→ Bonaire / Scuba Diving).* Of course, visitors can also enjoy *sailing* and *windsurfing.* Lac Bay is especially good for windsufing with shallow water making it appropriate for both beginners and advanced surfers.

Several hotel complexes like Divi Flamingo Beach Resort, the Sand Dollar Beach Club and the Sunset Beach Hotel have *tennis courts,* lit by floodlights, making it possible to play during the evening when it isn't as hot. Even non-guests can book tennis courts at the hotel reception. *Cycling* and *horseback riding* is possible on Bonaire as well.

Taxis

Taxi drivers wait for fares mostly at the airport. Otherwise, visitors will not see many taxis on Bonaire. Taxis do not cruise around seeking out passengers. If in need of a taxi, contact **Tel: 8100.** Taxi prices are set. Every taxi driver has a price list including prices for island tours.

Telephone

Placing international calls from Bonaire is no problem. To call Bonaire from Great Britain, dial 00 599 7 followed by the number; from the US and Canada, 011 599 7 and the number.

Time of Day → *Aruba / Time of Day*

Tourism Office

In contrast to tourist services on some other islands, the staff in Bonaire's two tourism offices go to great lengths to help each individual tourist.
Those with questions or in need of assistance should contact the following:

■ **On Bonaire**
Tourism Corporation Bonaire, Kaya Simon Bolivar 12, Kralendijk, Bonaire, Dutch Caribbean; Tel: +599 7 8322 or 8649, Fax: +599 7 9408

■ **In the Netherlands**
Tourism Office Bonaire, Visseringlaan 24, 2288 ER Rijswijk, Netherlands, Tel: +31 70 3954444, Fax: +31 70 3368333.

Travelling to Bonaire

Direct flights from Europe to Bonaire are scarce. Depending on the flight schedules, *KLM* offers flights to Bonaire from Amsterdam once or twice a month. There are many more flights to Bonaire if travellers are willing to stop over in Aruba (→ *Travelling to Aruba)* or Curaçao (→ *Travelling to Curaçao).* From either of these islands, there are several flights a day to Bonaire, offered by *ALM* or *Air Aruba.* Ferry service operating between the three islands on a regular basis has not yet been established.
When leaving Bonaire, an exit tax of $10 (£6) is charged at the airport.

Curaçao

General Information

Curaçao, the "Island of many faces" as it is lovingly called by its residents, it is the largest island in the Dutch Antilles with an area of 448 square kilometres (175 square miles). It stands out through its perpetual sunshine, the idyllic beaches and its pleasant climate thanks to the constant trade winds. Curaçao is also the southernmost of the Antilles and lies around 60 kilometres off the Venezuelan coast. Like Aruba and Bonaire, it is outside the hurricane belt.

Curaçao is 65 kilometres (41 miles) long and 11 kilometres (7 miles) wide at its widest point. A few hills protrude from the wavy volcanic landscape. In the island's northwestern regions is *Mount Christoffel,* the highest elevation reaching 375 metres (1,226 feet). On a clear day, it is possible to see Aruba, Bonaire and Venezuela from the summit.

Curaçao's landscape is characterised by the arid climate: bushes, cactuses reaching 6 metres (20 feet) and divi divi trees give Curaçao its special charm. The southern coast is punctuated by bays reaching far inland. On the largest of these, *Schottegat,* lies *Willemstad,* the island's capital city with one of the most beautiful harbours in the Caribbean.

Curaçao, famous through its liqueur, is also the governmental seat of the island group. Only Aruba has special status.

Accommodation

Curaçao has fourteen good to top-rate **hotels,** eight of which have their own beaches. There are also numerous smaller hotels which will suffice for those with lower expectations.

■ Private Accommodation

Those who would like to rent out a **private home** or **apartment** on Curaçao can contact the *Curaçao Hotel and Tourism Association (CHATA),* Tel: 63 62 60, or the → *Tourism Office* at Pietermaai 19 in Willemstad. These offices have current information on apartments, guest houses and smaller hotels.

■ Prices

The price for a simple double room start around $15 (£9) and go all the way to $50 or $60 (£30 or £36). Note that hotels often add 5% tax and 10% service charge to the bill. Sometimes, there is even an energy surcharge of $3 (£1.80) per day. Be sure to ask about these surcharges in advance.

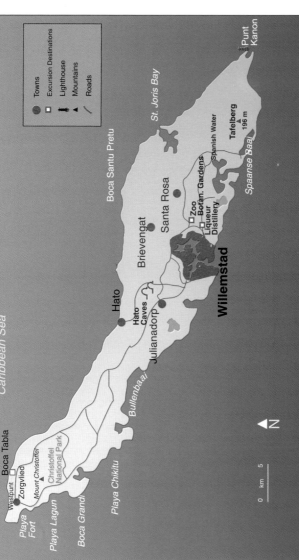

CURAÇAO

Towns
Excursion Destinations
Lighthouse
Mountains
Roads

Caribbean Sea

Boca Tabla
Westpunt
Zorgvlied
Playa Fort
Mount Christoffel
Christoffel National Park
Playa Lagun
Boca Grandi
Playa Chikitu

Bullenbaai

Hato
Hato Caves
Julianadorp

Brievengat
Santa Rosa

Boca Santu Pretu

St. Joris Bay

Zoo
Botan. Gardens
Liqueur Distillery

Willemstad

Spanish Water
Tafelberg
196 m
Spaanse Baai

Punt Kanon

N

0   km   5

■ Hotels

Those who prefer to stay in one of the fourteen **Luxury Hotels** should book from home. This is usually the less expensive option. All hotels have air conditioning, most have their own restaurants and cable television. Hotels offer guests shuttle service from the hotel to Willemstad. Hotels also have show and performances every evening. Those who would like to arrange their own accommodation on Curaçao can easily do this with a fax machine and a credit card. Don't accept the first price quoted; it is worth bargaining even during high season.

Curaçao's Hotels in the Upper Categories

Avila Beach Hotel, Penstraat 130-134; Tel: +599 9 614377, Fax: +599 9 611493
Classic, well preserved building from 1780, built as the governor's seat, with a new tract, stylish ambience, 85 rooms, private beach, restaurant, tennis courts, shops, baby-sitting service, some rooms with a kitchenette.

Club Seru Coral, Koraal Perier 10; Tel: +599 9 67 84 99, Fax: +599 9 678256
Brand new studio and bungalow complex in Curaçao's inland regions, with walls and security guards; 30 rooms, large swimming pool, children's pool, restaurant, bar, shops, laundry facilities, rooms with kitchenette.

Coral Cliff Hotel & Casino, Santa Marta Baai; Tel: +599 9 641820, Fax: +599 9 641781
In a quiet location, this hotel is off the beaten tourist track on the island's northerwestern coast (Santa Marta Baai), beautiful view of the sea, 35 studio apartments with kitchenette, private beach, restaurant, bar, shows, activities, baby-sitting service, tennis, scuba diving, water sports.

Curaçao Caribbean Resort & Casino, Piscaderea Baai; Tel: +599 9 625000, Fax: +599 9 625846
Luxury hotel on its own private bay, 10 minutes from Willemstad, 200 rooms with a balcony, private beach, swimming pool, restaurant, bars, disco, shows, casino, tennis courts, shops, activities, baby-sitting service, hair salon, convention and party rooms, water sports.

Curaçao Plaza & Casino, Plaza Piar; Tel: +599 9 612500, Fax: +599 9 618347Hotel in the centre of Willemstad within the walls of an old fort, 254 rooms, almost all with a view of the harbour or the sea, swimming pool, restaurant, bars, disco, casino, shops, activities, baby-sitting service.

Holiday Beach Hotel & Casino, Pater Euwensweg 31; Tel: +599 9 625400, Fax: +599 9 625409
An attractive hotel around five minutes from the pontoon bridge in Willemstad, 200 rooms with a balcony, private beach, swimming pool, restaurant, bars, disco, shows, casino, tennis courts, shops, activities, baby-sitting service, hair salon, convention and party rooms, water sports.

Airport Hotel Holland, Franklin D. Rooseveltweg 524; Tel: +599 9 81120
The hotel lies inland near the international airport. Ten minutes to the beach. 45 rooms, swimming pool, large terrace, restaurant, bars, disco, shows, casino, tennis courts, activities, baby-sitting service, water sports.

Las Palmas Hotel & Casino, Piscadera Baai; Tel: +599 9 625200, Fax: +599 9 625962
The 86 bungalows and 95 hotel rooms lie in the middle of a park, ten minutes from the centre of Willemstad. The bungalows have two bedrooms and their own kitchen. The complex is characterised by tropical gardens. Private beach, swimming pool, restaurant, bars, disco, shows, casino, tennis courts, shops, supermarket, activities, baby-sitting service, water sports.

Lions Dive Hotel & Marina, Bapor Kibra z/n; Tel: +599 9 618100, Fax: +599 9 625409
Near the underwater park, 72 rooms with a view of the sea. Has the best water sports facilities. Private beach, swimming pool, restaurant, bars, disco, shows, shops, activities, baby-sitting service, water sports.

Otrobanda Hotel & Casino, Breedestraat; Tel: +599 9 627400, Fax: +599 9 627299
A new hotel with a view of the harbour, 45 rooms, 2 restaurants, bar, shops, casino.

Porto Paseo Hotel & Casino, De Rouvilleweg 47; Tel: +599 9 627878, Fax: +599 9 627969
The hotel lies only a few metres from the centre of Willemstad. Swimming pool, tropical gardens, casino, water sports.

Princess Beach Resort, Dr. Martin Luther King Boulevard; Tel: +599 9 614944, Fax: +599 9 614131
The hotels is located near the underwater park with 202 rooms and 138 junior suites along Curaçao's most beautiful and longest beach. 74 rooms in bungalow style, some rooms with kitchenette, swimming pool, restaurant, bars, billiard room, tennis court, sauna.

Beaches and Swimming

There are only a few really good beaches on Curaçao. The northwestern coast is rugged and not suitable for swimming. However, the western coast offers a number of protected bays and beaches with excellent conditions for swimming and scuba diving. Many of the nicest beaches are privately owned and the owners charge $1.50 to $4.50 (90p to £2.70) for admission to the beach. In return for this, there are changing cabins, toilets and a small refreshment stand on the beach. No one really maintains the public beaches as can be seen from their appearance. Women should refrain from going topless on public beaches but this is tolerated on private beaches. The nicest beaches lie northwest of Willemstad.

■ The only beach near Willemstad belongs to the *Avila Beach Hotel*. Those not staying in this hotel must pay admission to the beach.

■ *Southeast of Willemstad,* near the Hotel Princess Beach, Lions Dive Hotel and at the Seaquarium lies an artificial beach 450 metres (around ¼ mile) in length. The beach has showers and toilets but it also costs admission.

■ Somewhat farther south lies another *private beach* near *Jan Thiel Bay.* Admission for tourists is free of charge, but there is a charge when entering by car.

■ *Northeast of Willemstad* are a number of small bays which are worth discovering. However, there is an admission charge for each bay even if it's a public beach.

■ In front of the *Coral Cliff Resort,* the beach is very clean and well maintained.

■ *Playa Abau* is very popular among local residents.

■ The beach near *Westpoint* below the church cannot be recommended. There is so much rubbish under the trees that it is no longer pleasant to linger there.

Eating in a very special ambiance: the "Pirate's Nest" on Aruba looks like a ship on the beach

Camping

In contrast to most other Caribbean islands, campers are not outright banned from Curaçao; there is even a camping area. It lies on the Spaanse Water Bay near Brakkeput. The address: Camping, Spanish Waters, Arowakenweg 41A, PO Box 3291, Tel: 67 44 28. One night costs at least $20 (£12). Camping is also allowed on some beaches, but there are no showers, toilets or fresh water there.

Car Rental

Those arriving at Curaçao's international airport will already be confronted with a number of car rental agencies. All have an official price list, making quick price comparisons possible. Prices range from $30 (£18) for a compact car to $40 (£24) for a jeep per day. This includes unlimited mileage and insurance.

To rent a car, a valid national driving licence and a deposit are required. The deposit can be taken care of by credit card. Avis, Budget, Europcar and others also rent out **motor scooters** and **motorcycles.**

On Curaçao, traffic is on the right-hand side of the road and traffic signs are international standard.

Driving on Curaçao — what to know

— Roads leading straight on have the right of way.
— If it does happen to rain on Curaçao, then the streets can become quite slippery due to dust on the roads.
— Jeep accidents are relatively common. Many jeep drivers underestimate the vehicle's high point of gravity in curves. If streets are slippery, jeeps can easily slide off the road.
— In case of an accident, drivers must stay with the vehicle until the police arrive.

Climate

As with the other two ABC islands, Curaçao has no seasons. It is always summer. The average temperature is almost 28°C (82.4°F) and the sea is just as warm. Throughout the year, the island has around 500 mm (19 inches) of precipitation, mostly in November and December (→ *Mosquitoes).* Despite the high temperatures and the low levels of precipitation, the climate on the "island of many faces" is quite pleasant thanks to the constant trade winds which bring a refreshing breeze.

Curaçao Liqueur

When the Spanish landed on the island during the 16th century, they brought hundreds of orange trees to Curaçao. However, the plants only produced small, bitter oranges due to the dry climate.

Ultimately, it was discovered that the peel contained aromatic oils if dried in the sun. This was then used in various drinks and foods. Today, the fruit is used to produce the famous liqueur. On the eastern end of the island, extensive orange groves produce the peel to be dried in the sun on special terraces.

The world famous Curaçao liqueur has been distilled by the "Senior & Co." distillery since 1896. This is the only company which may officially claim its product is 'authentic'. The distillery is housed in the historical *Cholobolo Landhuis* (or country estate house) near Willemstad. Visitors can visit the old yet very modern complex and of course, sample the liqueur. This original distillery produces the liqueur in clear, orange, amber, green and blue shades — the taste remains the same. Meanwhile, new flavours have been created: chocolate, coffee and raisin.

Customs Regulations → *Bonaire / Customs Regulations*

Drinking Water

The drinking water on Curaçao comes from large salt extraction plants. It is palatable at any time right from the tap. Sometimes, tap water is warm because some of the water pipes are only slightly below the ground or even above ground. If it tastes different from at home, this can be because it is very soft after coming from the salt extraction plants.

Be careful when drinking from wells. The source of the water is not apparent and is usually not of drinking quality.

Electricity

Visitors must count on power failures on Curaçao. Electrical appliances can run somewhat slower. The electrical current on the island is normally 110 to 130 volts. some hotels produce their own electricity with a current of 220 volts. Therefore it is a good idea to bring along electrical items which can be switched to accommodate different electrical currents. US standard adapters will prove very helpful.

Emergencies

Police: emergencies 114; or 66 61 00, 66 62 00 or 66 63 00
Fire Department: emergencies 114; or 44 44 44
Ambulance: emergencies 112; or 62 58 22 or 62 49 00 (hospital)

Entering Curaçao

Since one of the main sources of income for Curaçao is tourism, entry formalities for tourists, especially those from Europe and North America, are uncomplicated. The customs officials require a valid passport and a return or onward ticket upon arrival. A visa or proof of vaccination is not required. During the flight, tourists are given an entry card which should be filled out on the plane to avoid delays later in the airport. The passport is needed to fill this out so be sure to have this available during the flight.

Those planning on staying on the island longer than three months will need a visa. However, it is better to enter as a tourist and take care of this after arriving. Working on Curaçao is only possible with a work permit.

For tourists, Curaçao has something special upon arrival in the International Airport. Tourists can purchase duty-free alcoholic beverages and cigarettes in the arrivals hall.

Excursions

Similar to Aruba, Curaçao has numerous organisations offering excursions and island tours. On every street corner, in every bar and hotel, one will find flyers advertising the selection.

Tour Organisers on Curaçao

Taber Tours, Tel: 37 66 37; **Casper Tours,** Tel: 53 010; **Benchi Tours,** Tel: 61 86 60; **Curven Tours & Sightseeing,** Tel: 37 98 06 **Daltino Tours,** Tel: 61 48 88

A Selection of Tours and Excursions (Taber Tours)

Island Tour Eastern Curaçao, price: $10 (£6), children $5 (£3), lasting around three hours
Horseback Tour, $15 (£9) per person, 1½ hours
Island Tour Western Curaçao, $12.50 (£7.50), children $6.25 (£3.75)
Special Tour (East and West), $15 (£9), children $7.50 (£4.50), lasting around 5 hours

Day Tour to the Sea Aquarium, $16 (£9.60), children $10.50
(£6.30), lasting around 5 hours
Boat Tour by Sunset, $29.50 (£17.70), children $20 (£12), lasting
around 2 hours
Snorkelling Tour to Vaersenbai, with transport $35 (£21), lasting
around 5 hours
Combination Tour, $25 (£15), lasting around 6 hours
Coral Cliff Swimming Cruise, $40 (£24), children $27.50 (£16.50),
lasting around 7 hours

History

Curaçao was discovered by the Spaniard *Alonso de Ojeda* in July 1499.
Before this, the Arawak Indians had settled on the island, living predominantly
from fishing. The Spaniards annexed the island into their kingdom but — as
with Aruba and Bonaire — showed little interest in the *"Islas Inútiles",* the
"useless islands". The Spaniards had only a small garrison stationed on

*Not only beaches, palms and coral reefs... on the ABC islands, a Dutch
organ is almost a normal attraction*

Curaçao and left a few goats, sheep, donkeys and cattle behind for the Arawaks to tend. That was pretty much everything.

In April 1634, the Dutch West Indian Company, founded 13 years prior, decided to take Curaçao. Three months later, a fleet of six battleships under the command of *Johan van Walbek* entered Curaçao's harbour. Since the fleet was small, the Spaniards fled to Curaçao's western end where they could withstand the attack for a few months; then, they surrendered. From that point in time, Curaçao has been Dutch.

Governor Peter Struyvesant attempted to control the Caribbean from Curaçao and, under the direction of the Dutch West Indian Company, agriculture was spurred on. For this, slaves from Africa were needed and Curaçao soon became hub for slave trade. In 1654, numerous Dutch Jews who fled from Brazil came to the island. Trade with other islands and South America took another upswing.

Despite this, turbulent times would follow: in 1795, the slaves revolted on the Knip plantation. The uprising was quashed and 29 slaves were executed. The island had to increase its defence efforts externally as well: over time, the Dutch built a total of eight forts on Curaçao which were desperately needed to defend the populace from French and English pirates. In 1800, Curaçao was taken by the British. However, the Dutch fought back two years later. With the treaty of Paris in 1815 after the Napoleonic Wars, Curaçao was finally awarded to the Dutch.

When slavery was abolished in 1863, the economic difficulties in which large land owners found themselves grew more severe, many became impoverished and only 100 years later did Curaçao have an economic upswing: the first oil refinery was built on Curaçao, one of the largest in the world, mainly to process oil from Venezuela. Curaçao became one of the richest islands in the Caribbean, living standards improved enormously until this was halted with the oil crisis in the 1980s. Unemployment skyrocketed to 21 percent. When the shell corporation decided to give up the refinery, the government bought it and leased it to Venezuela. Even today, the economic prosperity of island residents is dependent on the oil industry. For example, the terminal near Bullenbai counts among the largest bunker harbours in the world.

Curaçao's second most important source of income is tourism. Up to 1983, it was mainly wealthy Venezuelans who visited this island 'on their doorstep'. However, when the Bolivar was drastically devalued in that very year, the number of Venezuelan visitors dropped just as dramatically by 70 percent. The government was forced to take over a number of hotels to protect the employees from being laid off. When the recession hit the US in the 1990s, causing the number of American tourists to drop, this was not as bad as it seemed. Curaçao had long since begun to step up their efforts in attracting Europeans to the island. In the past years, Curaçao has also been a popular port of call for cruise ships; the passengers visit the island for a few hours and leave some money on Curaçao in doing so.

Curaçao is famous throughout the world for its → *Curaçao liqueur* with the unusual blue colour. This is still produced in the Chobolobo factory from orange peel and exported throughout the world.

Holidays and Celebrations

All banks and stores remain closed on the following **official holidays:**

■ **January 1: New Year's Day**
The first of January is pretty much a day of recovery from the festivities of the previous night. New Year's Eve is celebrated on the streets, in the bars and hotels much like many other places in the world.

■ **February: Carnival / Mardi Gras**
Folklore groups perform typical dances in the hotels and on the streets. Dances include the *Baile di Sinta, Danza, Mazurka* and the *Tamba.* The large parade traditionally takes place Sunday morning on Curaçao, beginning at 10 am and lasting around three hours. Monday is a day of recovery, shops remain closed. Some even remain closed on Tuesday.

■ **April: Easter**
■ **The queen's birthday on April 30th is a traditional holiday in the Kingdom of the Netherlands, thus on Curaçao as well.**

■ **May 1: Labour Day**
This holiday is popular for a relaxing day at the beach.

■ **Christ's Ascension**

■ **July 2: Flag Day**

■ **December: Christmas**
Christmas is celebrated on the 25th and 26th of December on Curaçao.

International Press

There are several daily newspapers on Curaçao, two of which are in Dutch. In addition, there are Spanish newspapers and a free advertisement paper with a large editorial section in English. International English-language magazines are available in all the larger hotels.

Language → *Aruba / Language*

Leaving Curaçao

A departure tax is levied at the airport when leaving Curaçao. For flights to other islands in the Dutch Antilles, it is 10 NAF or around $6 (£3.60). Passengers with destinations outside the Dutch Antilles must pay around 18 NAF or $10 (£6).

Medical Care

Medical care on Curaçao is very good by Caribbean standards. The *physicians* have usually been educated in the United States or Europe. They can be reached at any time by contacting the hotel reception and hotels will usually have general practitioners and dentists under contract. In severe cases, there is the *St. Elizabeth Hospital* with 820 beds. The hospital (Tel: 624900) also has two decompression chambers for diving accidents and it is accessible in 20 minutes from anywhere on the island. There are also well-stocked *pharmacies* in every larger town.

Money

The same currency is used on Curaçao as on Bonaire, the *Netherlands Antilles guilder* (NAG or NAfl). The exchange rate to the US dollar is set, as on Aruba. One US dollar = 1.77 NAfl. It is possible to pay in US dollars everywhere. In contrast to shops, restaurants and hotels, the banks accept Eurocheques. Those who want to be liquid at all times should bring along traveller's cheques in US dollars.

Banks on Curaçao are usually open Monday to Friday from 8:30 to noon and 1 to 4:30 pm.

Most shops and all hotels and car rental agencies also accept credit cards like Mastercard (Eurocard), Visa and American Express. When renting a car, it is a good idea to pay by credit card so the deposit is taken care of.

Mosquitoes

The mosquitoes can become a real annoyance during the months of November and December but also sometimes in May and June — and this, even though insecticide is sprayed in the tourist centres. Two methods of defence are: bringing along insect repellent from home which only provides protection for a few hours, or hanging a mosquito net over the bed.

Nature

Curaçao's dry climate allows for only sparse vegetation. It only takes on a tropical character in a few places like surrounding the Kip Country Estate Hill or at around 200 metres (655 feet) in elevation around Mount St. Christoffel. Although it is repeatedly emphasised that around 500 different types of plants grow on Curaçao, this is not a lot.

However, there are dozens of different *cactuses, agaves* and *aloe plants* making for a botanically impressive sight. In addition to these are the *wild orchids* and the *divi divi tree* which always grows in the direction of the wind. Harmless *lizards* and *iguanas* as well as the *Curaçao deer* which was almost extinct at one point, are all typical of Curaçao's fauna. In the air and on tree branches, visitors can see several types of pygmy parrots like the *trupial* or prikichi, various kinds of *humming birds* and *reed warblers*.

Curaçao's idyllic beaches are one of the most impressive aspects of the "island with many faces"

Night Life

Those who enjoy the turbulence of night life with discos and pubs on Mediterranean islands like Mallorca will find that Curaçao is the wrong destination for them. Night life on Curaçao is much different.

Almost every larger hotel has its own casino. The reason is that the casinos generate the highest profits. In addition to this, night life takes place in the restaurants and bars in the various hotels which, of course, do their best to keep their guests in their hotel when spending money. In doing this, hotels have something special almost every evening — from happy hour to all-out shows. The restaurants which are not associated with hotels do their best to attract the tourists as well. You will hardly be able to save yourself from the flurry of advertising flyers promising the best in entertainment: this bar has a performance scheduled or that restaurant has the best show with dinner.

Another tip: *Birdland* near the Punda Arcades. Dutch and American music stars perform here; it offers its guests live music seven days a week.

The People of Curaçao

Around 150,000 people live on Curaçao, a cosmopolitan community. The original inhabitants, the Arawak Indians, have mixed with the African slaves who were brought from the Netherlands during the past century. Later, immigrants came to Curaçao from all over the globe. They were drawn by commerce and the oil industry. Today, around 80 nationalities are represented on Curaçao. Curaçao has a very high living standards.

Postal System

The postal system works well from Curaçao to Europe. The post office, *"Postkantoor"*, is located at Waaigatplein 1 in Willemstad, Punda district. A postcard to Europe costs one guilder; a letter, 2 or 3 guilders depending on the weight.

Restaurants

There are numerous good restaurants on Curaçao, serving all types of cuisine. It is not intended to single out any particular restaurants here since, as noted for restaurants on the other islands, the cooks change jobs frequently.

The following are the **addresses and telephone numbers for restaurants** listed according to type of cuisine. Reserving a table is definitely recommended; otherwise, there could be a substantial wait.

International Cuisine on Curaçao

American
Cactus Club, Van Stavenweg 6, Tel: 37 16 00

Arabian
El Sultan, Cas Coraweg 56a, Tel: 37 09 23

Argentinean
El Gaucho, Schottegatweg Oost 173, Tel: 60 18 87

Chilean
El Entablao, Indjuweg 47, Tel: 61 48 55

Chinese
Chun King, Wilhelminaplein 1, Tel: 61 18 55
Foon Yuen, Cas Coraweg, Tel: 37 85 59
Lam Yuen, Fokkerweg 25, Tel: 61 55 40
Rose Garden, Oude Caracasbaaiweg, Tel: 61 45 74
The Great Wall, Centro Commercial Antilia, Tel: 37 77 99
Yuen Tung, Castorweg 19, Tel: 61 54 87

Dutch
't Kokkeltje, Hotel Holland, Tel: 68 80 44
't Pannetje, Bloempot Shopping Centre, Tel: 37 08 74
De Sandwich Shop, Hanchi Snoa 22
De Koekepan, Sta. Rosaweg, Tel: 36 97 47

French
Bistro Le Clochard, Riffort, Tel: 62 56 66 / 62 56 67
La Bistroëlle, Promenade Shopping Centre, Tel: 37 69 29
Larousse, Penstraat 5, Tel: 65 54 18
Zeelandia Restaurant, Polarisweg, Tel: 61 46 88

Indonesian
Garuda, Curaçao Caribbean Hotel, Tel: 62 65 19
Landhuis Brievengat, Tel: 37 83 44
Rijstafel Indonesia, Mercuriusstraat 13, Tel: 61 26 06
Surabaya, Waterfortboog, Tel: 61 73 88
Surindo, Uranusstraat 5, Tel: 61 54 85

International
Alouette, Orionweg 12, Zeelandia, Tel: 61 82 22
Andre Meijer, Rio Canarioweg, Tel: 44 666

Balau Terrace, Curaçao Seaquarium, Tel: 61 66 66
Belle terrace, Avila Beach Hotel, Penstraat 130, Tel: 61 43 77
Caribean Breeze, Waterfortboog, Tel: 61 69 18
De Taveerne, Landhuis Groot Davelaar, Tel: 37 06 69
Down Town Terrace, Gomez Plaza, Tel: 61 67 22
Fort Nassau, Tel: 61 30 86
Fort Waakzaamheid, Berg Domi, Tel: 62 36 33
Guacamaya Steakhouse, Schottegatweg West 365, Tel: 65 75 58
Restaurant Club Seru Coral, Koraal Partier 10, Tel: 67 84 99
Grill King, Waterfortboog 2, Tel: 61 68 70
Queen's View, Sorsaka Chiki, Tel: 67 51 05
Paradis, Colon Shopping Centre, Tel: 62 62 66
Pinocchio's, Promenade Shopping Centre, Tel: 37 04 08
Percy's Food, Caracasbaaiweg 56, Tel: 61 57 67
Rodeo Ranch, Curaçao Seaquarium, Tel: 61 57 57
Rum Runners, De Rouvilleweg 9F, Tel: 62 30 38
Seaview Restaurant, Waterfortboog, Tel: 61 66 88
Sizzy, Saliña 163F, Tel: 61 77 07
The Wine Cellar, Concordiastraat, Tel: 61 21 78
Tropical Treat, Sta. Rosaweg 194, Paseata, Tel: 67 75 37
Zeelandia, Landhuis Zeelandia, Polarisweg 28, Tel: 61 46 88

Italian
Baffo & Bretalla, Curaçao Seaquarium, Tel: 61 87 00
Copzzoli's Pizza, Breedestraat 27
Il Barile, Hanchi Snoa 12, Tel: 61 34 82
La Pergola, Waterfortboog 12, Tel: 61 34 82
Pizza Hut, Schottegatweg West 193, Tel: 61 61 61

Local Cuisine
Golden Star, Socratesstraat 2, Tel: 54 795
Calypso, Pietermaai 25, Tel: 61 71 80
Chez Susanne, Blomonteweg 1, Tel: 68 85 45
Finca Mar Restaurant, Lagoen K-27, Tel: 64 13 77
Funchipot, Landhuis Jan Kock, Tel: 64 80 87
Janchie's Restaurant, Westpunt 15, Tel: 64 01 26
Martha Koosje, Martha Koosje 10, Tel: 64 82 35
Nubia Restaurant, Columbusstraat, Tel: 61 66 06
Oasis, Savonet 79 Banda Abao, Tel: 64 00 85
Playa Forti, Westpunt, Tel: 62 03 45
Caribana, De Rouvilleweg, Tel: 62 03 45
My Way Restaurant & Bar, Dr. M. L. King Blvd. 93, Tel: 65 75 58

Greek
Kreta Eetcafé, S. B. N. Doormanweg, Tel: 37 06 85

Mexican
Rodeo Ranch / South of the Border, Curaçao Seaquarium, Tel: 61 57 57
Alapari, Texas Style, Saliña

Portuguese
Porto Madeire, Fokkerweg 3, Tel: 65 61 11

Danish
Belle Terrace, Penstraat 130, Tel: 61 43 77

Fish and Seafood
Cést la vie, Goseiweg 148, Tel: 36 98 35
El Marinero, Schottegatweg 87b, Tel: 37 98 33
Fisherman's Wharf, Dr. M. L. King Blvd., Tel: 65 75 58
Pices Seafood Restaurant & Bar, Caracasbaaiweg 476, Tel: 67 281
Villa Elizabeth, Koraalspechtweg 1, Tel: 65 75 65

When looking through the menu, be sure to not whether the 10% **service charge** is included in the prices. If not, it will be added to the bill. Another five percent for good service will certainly be appreciated by the wait staff.

Scuba Diving

The seas surrounding Curaçao are home to numerous fish, living in the crystal clear waters at 24 to 27°C (75 to 81°F). Curaçao rests on volcanic stone on which coral lime built up over millennia. Only a few metres from the coast lie beautiful coral reefs. In addition to these are numerous shipwrecks. All told, there are around 1,000 diving sites surrounding Curaçao, waiting to be discovered.
Generally speaking, the first underwater 'terrace' is at a depth of around 10 metres (33 feet) which falls off at an angle of 45° to the seafloor. Visibility is around 24 metres (78 feet) on average.
There are countless diving shops on the island. Price comparisons are worth the effort.

Diving Areas
Three diving areas are especially good: In 1983, the **Curaçao Underwater Park** was established. It extends from the Princess Hotel to East Point. The park stretches from the coast up to a depth of 60 metres (around 200 feet). Sixteen buoys were anchored on the seafloor so that boats must not drop anchor, potentially harming the coral. There are only a few places in this diving

area which are accessible from the beach; most are reached by boat. Harpoons and spears are not allowed in the park; divers may not remove any coral or aquatic animals.

The **second** diving area lies between the Princess Beach Hotel and the Bullenbaai and is called *Central Curaçao;* the **third** diving area extends from West Point to the lighthouse on Cape St. Marie. The *Guide to the Curaçao Underwater Park* by Jeffrey Sybesman & Tom Van't Hof offers a good overview of the park's diving areas. This book is available in all bookstores and diving shops on the island.

Shopping

Curaçao is a commercial hub in the Caribbean. Almost everything can be found on the island. 99 percent of the shops are located in the capital city of Willemstad, which is relatively large by Caribbean standards with a population of 145,000.

Despite the size of Willemstad, those shops, stores and sights which are interesting for tourists are all within a five-minute walk, within five blocks of the business centre of Punda — between the Sha Capriles Kade at the Floating Market, the Columbusstraat, the Bredestraat and the Handelskade. Hundreds of shops can be found here, some streets are just five metres (16 feet) wide and on both sides, numerous items can be found in the shops at surprisingly low prices. Worth mentioning are the jewellery shops with gems and jewellery which is unparalleled in the Caribbean.

Shops are open Monday to Saturday from 8 am to noon and 2 to 6 pm. When cruise ships dock in the harbour, then shops will also open, with the exception of grocery stores.

Sights

Two factors characterise Curaçao's western regions and with this, the sights worth seeing: climate and history. The dry climate makes for arid landscapes and the historical events gave rise to several historical buildings. However, the natural beauties are the more attractive of the two.

■ Christoffel Park

Christoffel Park lies in the island's western regions and was named after *Mount Christoffel* which reaches and elevation of 375 metres (1,226 feet) and offers a beautiful view of the island. The park comprises three former plantations, of which the *Landhuis Savonet* has remained preserved. The landscape is similar to that of Aruba: dry, reddish soil, numerous cactuses, aloe plants, orchids and occasionally a divi divi tree.

The three plantations — *Savonet, Zorgvlied* and *Zevenbergen* are the points of departure for three driving routes through Christoffel Park. The routes are well signposted and marked in different colours.

The Blue Route: The blue route is 9 kilometres (5½ miles) long and leads through the *Rooi Berú Valley,* the *Saliña* and *Boca Grandi* along to the limestone plateaux on the northern coast. The caves can be visited here (→ *below).*

The Green Route: The green route is 7.5 or 12 kilometres (4½ or 7½ miles) long and leads around Mount Christoffel. It offers beautiful views of the northern coast and the valleys. This tour is predestined for nature lovers. The wild bromilia and orchids at the higher elevations are especially impressive.

The Yellow Route and the Red Hiking Trail: The yellow route is 11 kilometres (7 miles) long. And then there is also a red hiking trail leading up Mount Christoffel, taking around three hours. With an experienced guide (demand is increasing so more and more guides are being trained) the hike starts at 9 am at the park entrance. The tour leads to Savonet / Boca Grandi. Hikers get a good impression of the old plantation system and the difficulty involved in the various irrigation methods, many wells, dams, rain collection basins and cisterns in coaxing some fertility out of nature. Hikers will be able to experience quite a lot of the strange flora and fauna up close.

The Deer Reserve: Another attraction this park has to offer is the deer reserve, founded a few years ago within a scientific research project involving the endangered Biná, the Curaçao deer. From an elevated platform and lead by an experienced guide, visitors can observe these rare and very shy creatures. (Be sure to make advance reservations by phoning Tel: 64 03 63.)

Other Sights in the Park: By no means should visitors miss seeing the breathtaking **caves** on the "blue route". Nearby, visitors can admire the *Indian rock drawings:* these drawings in black, white and okra are between 500 and 2,000 years old.

Thousands of rare bats hang from the ceiling in the *Kueba Bosé Caves* during the day. Because of the bats, the caves are not open to the general public but there are guided tours every day around 1 pm. One of the caves is around 125 metres (410 feet) long and very low at the entrance; visitors must crawl in.

The **Landhuis Savonet Plantation** from the 17th century lies at the entrance to Christoffel Park on Westpoint Road. It is, however, closed to the general public. Housed in a side building is a small **museum** with an exhibition on the geological history of Curaçao. Admission to the museum is 2.50 NAfl, and 1.50 NAfl per person for groups.

Admission to the Park and Opening Times: The park is open Monday to Saturday from 8 am. The entrance in the island's interior closes at 3 pm and at 4 pm on the ocean side. Of course, visitors may stay longer than this. Sundays, the park opens at 6 am and closes at 5 pm. Guided tours are possible at any time on request (Tel: 64 03 63).

■ Hato Caves

A visit to Hato Cave is also an impressive experience — stalactites and stalagmites, rock paintings dating back around 1,500 years, petrified coral and underground streams with small waterfalls. The limestone caves of Hato near the airport are the largest on the island with a total area of 4,900 square metres (48,070 square feet or a little over 3 square miles). They are open daily, except Mondays, from 10 am to 5 pm. Guided tours are offered: information and reservations, Tel: 68 03 79. Admission costs $4.50 (£2.70) for adults and $2.75 (£1.65) for children.

■ Botanical Gardens and Zoo

On the former *Cos Corá* plantation is now a botanical garden with the only (small) zoo in the Dutch Antilles. Visitors can see lions, bears, apes, deer, snakes and zebras. A playground was set up for the small guests with a souvenir shop right next door for the bigger guests. The botanical gardens and zoo are open from 9 am to 5:30 pm; admission is free of charge.

■ The Forts

To protect the island from pirate attacks or attacks from the English, Spanish or Dutch (depending on who was in power at the time) a number of forts were built on the island. These forts, *Fort Amsterdam, Fort Waaksaamheid, Fort Nassau* and the *Riffort,* can be visited free of charge.

Fort Amsterdam now houses a governmental seat. And — so they say — there is still a cannonball stuck in the church wall which was shot from Captain Bligh's Bounty in 1804. Inside Fort Amsterdam's church is an *ecclesiastical museum.* In the display cases are songbooks, baptismal gowns, costumes, antique silver chalices, old bibles and prayer books. The museum is open Monday to Friday from 10 am to noon and 2 to 5 pm. Admission is $2 (£1.20) for adults, $1 (60p) for children.

■ The Brewery

Not only liqueur fans but beer lovers will get their money's worth on Curaçao. The *Amstel Brewery* has set up a subsidiary on Curaçao, in which beer is brewed using the purified sea water. The other ingredients are imported from the Netherlands. The brewery is located on Rijkseenheid Boulevard, open for

Fisherman's Hut (Aruba) not only offers excellent windsurfing but the opportunity to observe the brown pelican up close

tours Tuesdays and Thursdays from 10 am to noon (samples of beer are also offered). If interested, contact the brewery in advance by phoning Tel: 61 29 44.

■ The Synagogue

Near Hanchi Snoa in Willemstad lies one of the island's special sights, the *Mikvé Israel-Emanuel Synagogue* from 1732 — the oldest synagogue in the western world. The large brass chandeliers with candles which are only lit on major holidays are said to be 300 years older than the synagogue itself, The chandeliers originate from Spain and Portugal. The sand which is traditionally strewn on the floor every day is to remind the worshippers of the wanderings of the Israelites through the Egyptian desert; it also served to dampen the worshippers' footsteps when they were prosecuted during the Inquisition. The synagogue is open to visitors from 9 to 11:45 am and from 2:30 to 7 pm. Admission to the synagogue is free of charge; donations are gladly accepted, no photographs allowed. Services are Friday evenings at 6:30 pm and Sunday mornings at 10 am.

The **Jewish Museum** is housed in two buildings from the 18th century situated in the synagogue's gardens. On display here is a collection of religious items which were donated by local families. The museum is closed on Jewish and legal holidays; otherwise, it is open Monday to Friday from 9 to 11:45 am and from 2:30 to 5 pm. Admission is $2 (£1.20).

■ The Floating Market

The floating market in the canal which leads to the Waaigat Yacht Harbour in Willemstad is also worth visiting. This floating market is composed of a number of colourful ships from Venezuela, Columbia and Curaçao. Of course, fresh fish is on sale here as well as tropical fruits and a number of small souvenirs sold right on board the ships. It is best to visit the market early in the morning since the fish and fruits are especially fresh then and the colourful market is more vibrant in the early morning sunlight.

■ The Floating Queen Emma Bridge

The floating Queen Emma Bridge is another attraction in Willemstad. It spans St. Anna Bay and connects the two districts of Punda and Otrabanda (meaning as much as "the other side"). The bridge is built from 16 large pontoons and is swung to the side around thirty times every day to let the ships pass in and out of the harbour. The present-day bridge was built in 1939, but it had two predecessors.

■ Otrobanda

The impressive historical district of Otrobanda in Willemstad's western regions can be explored in the company of a guide. When doing this, visitors will be told an anecdote or true story in connection with almost every building, making for an interesting and entertaining way to become familiar with this district.

The guided tour begins every Thursday at 5:15 pm at the Queen Emma Bridgehead in Otrabanda. The tour lasts around one hour and fifteen minutes and costs 10 NAfl (including one beverage).
Reservations are requested, Tel: 61 35 54.
Even more detail is offered by a tour through the historical Old Otrobanda district which takes visitors back to Curaçao of the 18th and 19th centuries, leading through romantic alleyways with old, weathered monuments to a glorious past. The tour guide presents examples of architecture from that period that would otherwise go unnoticed by many. The historical tour begins every Wednesday afternoon at 5:15 pm at the large clock on Brionplein across from the pontoon bridge. The price is 10 NAfl. Reservations are recommended, Tel: 37 87 17.

■ The Curaçao Museum
Founded in 1946, the Curaçao Museum lies on Van Leeuwenhoekstraat in the Otrabanda district. In the historical building from 1853 which was a quarantine station at that time, visitors can see antique furnishings, paintings and historical land and nautical maps of Curaçao and the Caribbean. The museum is open Tuesday to Saturday from 9 am to noon and 2 to 5 pm; Sundays from 10 am to 4 pm; closed Mondays.

■ The Coin Gallery
Coin collectors will be interested in a visit to Curaçao's Coin Gallery at Breetestraat 1. There, visitors can view a valuable coin collection but also a collection of bank notes and an exhibit of over 500 precious stones. The Coin Gallery is open Monday to Friday from 9 am to noon and 2 to 5 pm. Admission is free of charge, Tel: 61 36 00.

■ The Seaquarium
The Seaquarium is a special attraction on Curaçao. When else can one stand eye to eye with a shark on the other side of a thick plate of glass? Close encounters with a sea turtle — it is all possible in the Seaquarium near the Bapor Kibra shipwreck. The aquatic zoo provides an overview of Curaçao's underwater world with over 400 species. The Seaquarium directly behind the Lions Dive Hotel is open daily from 9 am to 10 pm. Admission is $6 (£3.60) for adults and $3 (£1.80) for children under 15, seniors over 63 and everyone who arrives after 6 pm.

Sports and Recreation

The main emphasis on Curaçao is on scuba diving *(→ Curaçao / Scuba Diving),* even though there are a lot of other sports and recreational activities that Curaçao has to offer. Aquatic sports top the list. But first other types of sports:

■ **Horseback Riding** is offered at Rancho Alegre, Tel: 81 181. An excursion on horseback costs $15 (£9) per hour. *Ashari's Ranch,* Groot Piscadera Kaya A-23, Tel: 86 254, also offers horseback tours.

■ Tourists can play **golf** at the *Curaçao Golf and Squash Club,* Wilhelminalaan in Emmastad. The club has a 9-hole golf course; green fee is $15 (£9) for 18 holes. Guests are allowed to play from 8 am to 12:30 pm. The club also has two squash courts. For $7 (£4.20) guests can play squash between 8 am and 6 pm. The Curaçao Golf and Squash Club can be reached by phoning Tel: 73 590.

■ Visitors can play **tennis** at *Santa Catharina Sport and Country Club* which has six hard courts, Tel: 67 70 28. Furthermore, most of the large hotels have their own tennis courts available to hotel guests. Be sure to bring along your own racquet and tennis balls.

■ **Jogging** is increasing in popularity on Curaçao. The best time for a jog is early in the morning when the temperatures are bearable and it is already light. During the evening hours, temperatures are relatively high and joggers could be surprised by the sudden nightfall.

■ Truly everything in the way of **water sports** is available to tourists on Curaçao: windsurfing, snorkelling, sailing, water skiing and jetskiing are all offered by larger hotels and on some of the public beaches.

The *Coral Cliff Diving School* also offers sailing courses with qualified instructors. The basic course is held in Santa Monica Bay. Advanced courses use larger boats and a coastal yacht is available for the course on "coastal navigation". Those who complete the final course receive international certification which enables them to rent out sailing yachts world-wide.

Sail courses are also offered at the *Sail Curaçao B.V.* sailing centre, Asiento Yacht Club, Brakkeput/Spaanse Water, Tel: 67 60 03.

Taxis

Taxis can be easily recognised by the sign on the roof and the 'TX' on the licence plates. Taxi stands can be found at the airport, in front of all the larger hotels and in many places around Willemstad. However, it is sometimes difficult to get a taxi in Willemstad itself. A taxi can be ordered by phoning **Tel: 61 67 11**. Complaints can be registered by phoning Tel: 61 55 77; to identify which taxi, the licence plate number is needed.

Telephone

International phone calls on Curaçao are just as simply placed as at home but are much more expensive. Therefore, it is best to have people call back.

■ Dialling Codes
International dialling code for Curaçao: (international access code +) 599 9 followed by the number.

Time of Day → *Bonaire / Time of Day*

Tourism Office

Curaçao has excellent tourist information services. The staff takes time to help each individual tourist. This has shown success: each year, the number of tourists to visit Curaçao increases significantly. Most tourists are between 25 and 34 years of age and stay on Curaçao from two to three weeks.

Curaçao's Tourism Offices

United States Representation
400 Madison Ave., Suite 311
New York, NY 10017
Tel: (212) 751-8266

Curaçao Tourism Officein Europe
Vasteland 82-84
PO Box 23 227
NE-3001 KE Rotterdam, Netherlands
Tel: +31 10 414 2639
Fax: +31 10 413 6834

**Curaçao Tourism
Development Bureau**
Pietermaai 19
Willemstad, Curaçao
Netherlands Antilles
Tel: +599 9 616000
Fax: +599 9 612305

A Great Service

On Curaçao, a special service has been established for tourists. Those walking around Willemstad's district of Punda will notice men and women in bordeaux coloured suits.

They not only supervise parking areas but also help tourists in all types of situations.

These are employees of the **Curaçao Hospitality Service,** CHS for short.

Whether in need of a doctor, shopping tips or information on tours, these people will help in any way they can. CHS employees speak English, Dutch, Spanish and Papiamento.

The CHS office is located at Passatstraat 18b, Tel: 61 79 91.

Travelling to Curaçao

KLM offers direct flights to Curaçao up to twice a week depending on the current flight schedule. In addition, KLM and Condor have flights every day to Curaçao via Aruba (→ *Aruba / Flights*).

Since autumn of 1994, *LTU* offers flights to Curaçao once every week, costing around DM 1,400 (£560). From the US, flight connections to Curaçao are good.

However, most North and South American airlines offer service to Aruba.

Vaccinations

Curaçao is free from malaria and there aren't any other infectious diseases on the island. Therefore, no vaccinations are required for visitors arriving from North America or Europe.